The
Bodhisattva Vow

The
Bodhisattva Vow

by
Geshe Sonam Rinchen

Translated and edited by
Ruth Sonam

Snow Lion
Boston & London

Snow Lion
An imprint of Shambhala Publications, Inc.
Horticultural Hall
300 Massachusetts Avenue
Boston, Massachusetts 02115
www.shambhala.com

Library of Congress Cataloging-in-Publication Data
Sonam Rinchen, 1933–
The Bodhisattva vow / by Geshe Sonam Rinchen; translated and
edited by Ruth Sonam.
p. cm.
Includes the text of Candragomin's Bodhisattvasaṃvaraviṃśaka
in English and Tibetan.
Includes bibliographical references.
ISBN 978-1-55939-150-4
1. Vows (Buddhism) 2. Bodhisattva (The concept) 3. Compassion
(Buddhism) 4. Buddhism—Prayer-books and devotions—English.
I. Sonam, Ruth, 1943– II. Candragomin. Bodhisattvasaṃvara-
viṃśaka. English and Tibetan. III. Title.
BQ4355.S66 2000
294.3′5—dc21
00-033842

Contents

Acknowledgment

I would like to thank my editor Susan Kyser for her assistance.

Chapter One

The Heart of Mahayana Practice

When we study and practice according to any complete presentation of the stages of the path leading to enlightenment, we should not consider the insights associated with the most limited and intermediate levels of spiritual capacity as distinct from those cultivated by people with the greatest capacity,[1] since these insights are basic and essential to all Mahayana practices. A Mahayana practitioner focuses on them with concern for the well-being of all living creatures.

It is not sufficient for a teaching to belong to the Great Vehicle. Those who teach it and those who study and practice it should be motivated by the wish to gain enlightenment for the sake of all living beings.

Atisha's *Lamp for the Path to Enlightenment*[2] succinctly summarizes the three levels of capacity, reminding us that anything done for the well-being of this life is not even considered an authentic practice of the Buddha's teaching. For a practice to be authentic it should be orientated towards future lives. The practices of those whose capacity is limited concentrate on developing strong refuge in the Three Jewels and a firm conviction regarding the connection between actions and their effects.

The practices of those with an intermediate capacity center on the understanding that any condition within cyclic existence is fraught with one kind of suffering or another. These practitioners focus on the attainment of liberation from this state through the three kinds of higher training—in ethical discipline, concentration and wisdom. Although liberation is possible as a result of familiarizing ourselves with an experiential understanding of the four noble truths,[3] this will not fulfill our highest potential nor will we be able to help others in the most effective way. Therefore, ideally, we should leave aside the paths of Hearers and Solitary Realizers,[4] embarking from the outset in the Great Vehicle bound for complete enlightenment with the intention to free all beings from their suffering, which we have come to understand well by first considering our own condition. Through the development of the altruistic intention we can accomplish all our short- and long-term aims without the need for austere practices.

What kind of person has the capacity to engage in the practices of the Great Vehicle? Those whose aim is restricted to personal liberation lack the necessary mental strength. Just to be concerned with the alleviation of our own suffering and the acquisition of happiness does not set us apart from animals, since they do as much.

The sun and moon give light to the earth. They do it without prejudice or pride and are never discouraged by their task. The earth willingly supports everything animate and inanimate upon it without considering it a burden. It does not feel dismayed if something is taken from it, nor delighted when something is deposited in it. A true practitioner of the Great Vehicle considers it no burden to accept personal responsibility for others but does so willingly.[5] A Bodhisattva is not discouraged by the task of trying to help all living beings to find happiness and gladly works for all without any prejudice. We should honestly ask ourselves whether we are or even wish to be like this. Hearing or reading about it should at least make us want to become more kind and helpful.

THE BENEFITS OF DEVELOPING THE ALTRUISTIC INTENTION

The altruistic intention is what turns us into Mahayana practitioners, genuine practitioners of the Great Vehicle. Our enthusiasm to develop the altruistic intention needs to become as great as a child's enthusiasm for play. Considering the many advantages it brings will give us the incentive to develop it. Shantideva devotes the first chapter of his *Way of the Bodhisattva*[6] to this. In his *Great Exposition of the Stages of the Path*[7] Je Tsongkhapa mentions the following ten benefits of developing the altruistic intention:

1. *It is the sole way into the Great Vehicle.* The altruistic intention is the deciding factor. If our wish to become enlightened in order to help all living beings is superficial, we are only seeming practitioners of the Great Vehicle. No matter how great our knowledge is or how intensively we practice even the two stages of tantra,[8] without the altruistic intention we will never attain enlightenment. We cannot even reach the Mahayana path of accumulation,[9] nor will what we are doing count as a Mahayana practice. On the other hand, someone with the altruistic intention but with no other special abilities is creating the cause for complete enlightenment and is performing a Bodhisattva practice by saying just one mantra or giving a handful of food to an animal. In the *Precious Garland* Nagarjuna[10] reminds his friend the king that if he wants to become enlightened, the basic requirement is the altruistic intention to do so for others' sake and that he must make it as firm and unshakable as Mount Meru, the king of mountains:

> If you and the world want to attain
> Unsurpassable enlightenment,
> Its roots are the altruistic intention,
> As stable as the king of mountains,
> Compassion that reaches every quarter
> And wisdom that does not rely on duality.

Without this intention, visualizing deities and celestial mansions is just like a tourist visiting a temple. With only the wish for freedom from cyclic existence and an understanding of the correct view, our tantric practice can yield no more than personal liberation. This is a misuse of the highest practices, which can bring complete enlightenment. Without the wish for freedom from cyclic existence, the altruistic intention, and the correct understanding of reality, intensive tantric practice and strong identification with the deity may even lead to rebirth as a demon. One great master said that without these three, completion stage practices focusing on the energy channels and winds are just like using a pair of bellows.

2. One is called a "Child of the Conquerors." No matter what other abilities one possesses—one may have clairvoyance or have an excellent understanding of the five fields of knowledge,[11] one may have understood emptiness and overcome the obstructions to liberation posed by the disturbing attitudes and emotions—one will never be called a Bodhisattva without the altruistic intention. But with it, even if one has no other accomplishments, even as an animal, one is a Bodhisattva. When a new Bodhisattva comes into being, the earth, which is the result of past actions performed collectively by its inhabitants, trembles to mark the arrival of one who will help free them from cyclic existence. The thrones of the enlightened ones shake, and there is jubilation like the rejoicing which greets the birth of an heir to a great monarch.

With tears in his eyes the great master Drubkang Gelek Gyatso advised his disciple Purchok Ngawang Jampa[12] to make the altruistic intention his main practice. He told him that his own teacher Rengo Azara had always insisted that the altruistic intention was the heart of the path to enlightenment and that the practices of the initial and intermediate levels were the means of giving birth to that intention, while practice of the six perfections and of tantra were the ways to strengthen and enhance it.

Once Drubkang Gelek Gyatso went to visit Rengo Azara, who was seated outside his cave near a thorn bush, engrossed in what he was reading. As Drubkang Gelek Gyatso approached him, he observed that sometimes Rengo Azara looked very pleased and exclaimed, "Well done, well done!" At other times he looked despondent and on the verge of tears. Later, when he enquired about this, Rengo Azara told him that he had been reading stories about the Buddha's past lives.[13] At times he was moved and delighted by the Buddha's great feats for the benefit of others while he was still a Bodhisattva. At other times he couldn't control his tears when he thought about his own behavior and the miserable condition of living beings, our mothers.

If great practitioners like him were so conscious of all their actions, we can surmise how important it is always to examine our conduct and thoughts. If they match those of such fine practitioners, we can rest easy. If they don't, we can see clearly what needs to be changed.

When Drubkang Gelek Gyatso was ready to go into retreat he paid a final visit to his master. Rengo Azara said, "I know you must go but I shall miss you. These days it is so rare to find anyone with whom to talk about the altruistic intention, but with you I can, and it always makes my heart feel light." He told Drubkang Gelek Gyatso to make sure that he developed the altruistic intention and gained experience of it. Drubkang Gelek Gyatso jokingly replied to his master, "I am something functional and so is the altruistic intention, which means that we can produce each other."[14] Later he was able to say, "In the mountains the altruistic intention is with me. In the valleys the altruistic intention is with me. It never leaves me wherever I go, whatever I do."

In fact, the altruistic intention is the essence of the Buddha's eighty-four-thousand different teachings which are the medicine for all our ills.[15] We need more than a detached interest in it. Only if we are fired by a real wish to become a Bodhisattva, or simply to become more kindhearted, will we make an effort to discover the way.

3. *One outshines Hearers and Solitary Realizers from the point of view of lineage or disposition.* As long as one has this special

wish and such an all-encompassing mental attitude, even if
no effort is made to develop it further, one is and remains a
Bodhisattva, just as a diamond, even if fragmented, remains
a diamond and is superior to any kind of gold jewelry. The
merit created by the altruistic intention surpasses all that
created by Hearers and Solitary Realizers. The light of the
stars is made insignificant by the sun's light. The sun does
not outshine them through any competitiveness nor does it
destroy their light. Just as finding a precious diamond can
rescue us from poverty, the altruistic intention removes the
poverty of the world. Wherever the great Indian master
Atisha traveled in Tibet, he always encouraged everyone to
give up their preoccupation with this life and to develop the
altruistic intention.

4. *One becomes a supreme field of offering.* This does not happen easily because it is not at all easy to develop the altruistic intention. It took Atisha twelve years. The Kadampa
masters[16] used to say that everyone had their own particular deity to visualize and a mantra to say, but the reason
why their practice didn't bear fruit was because they didn't
have the altruistic intention in their heart. We should at least
aim to create strong imprints so that in future it will take
only a small circumstance to make us develop the altruistic
intention.

It is said that King Ajatashatru[17] had strong imprints for
understanding emptiness which were activated in the following way: one day he invited Manjushri for a meal and
was just about to offer him a very fine garment he had made
ready, when Manjushri disappeared. Feeling very disap-
pointed, Ajatashatru put on the garment himself and mo-
mentarily also disappeared. As a result of this he gained
understanding of emptiness.

The gods Brahma and Indra pay homage to Bodhisattvas,
bless them to become more radiant and splendid and lend
their support to everything they do. The Buddha said that if
we want to pay homage to him, we should pay homage to

Bodhisattvas. As a mark of how much Buddhas value Bodhisattvas, it is said that if there were no one else to do it, a Buddha would fasten the leather thongs of a chariot round his own crown protrusion to pull it for a Bodhisattva who wished to ride out in search of sensual pleasure.

The *Gandavyuha Sutra* says, "Child of the family, the altruistic intention is like the seed for everything associated with Buddhahood."[18] What does this mean? Soil, water, heat and manure act as generic causes for rice, wheat and barley seedlings. The exclusive causes for each of these are the rice seed, the wheat seed and the barley seed. Only the specific cause combined with a variety of generic causes gives rise to a specific result. If the altruistic intention is the seed of enlightenment, the understanding of emptiness is a generic cause, which, like a mother, produces exalted beings of all three vehicles.

The Great Vehicle is distinguished from the other two on the basis of skillful means and not with regard to philosophical view. The altruistic intention is the preeminent feature of the Great Vehicle. Hearers and Solitary Realizers are engaged in extricating themselves from one extreme—that of worldly existence. They do so by understanding the nature of reality. Focusing on this they develop a combination of calm abiding and special insight, through which they can liberate themselves from cyclic existence. Practitioners of the Great Vehicle must avoid the other extreme, namely that of solitary peace. They do this by cultivating compassion and the altruistic intention. Nevertheless, skillful means and wisdom must be cultivated together because only their combination will produce enlightenment, just as both parents are needed to produce a child.

5. *Great merit is easily created.* Since every action of a Bodhisattva's life is directed towards alleviating the suffering of living beings and leading them to supreme happiness, how could this not create vast merit? Imagine providing the greatest comfort and the finest clothes and

jewels to countless people for an incalculable length of time. If this action were not accompanied by the altruistic intention, the merit from it, though great, would eventually come to an end. It would not be a Bodhisattva practice nor act as a cause for enlightenment. However, a mere handful of food given with the altruistic intention will create inexhaustible merit, constitute a Bodhisattva activity and act as a cause of enlightenment.

Why is the merit created by any action performed with the altruistic intention so vast? Because each action done for the sake of all living beings produces merit as limitless as those beings. We all long for happiness and well-being. This results from positive energy and there is no more powerful way of creating it than through the altruistic intention. In the *Way of the Bodhisattva* Shantideva says:

> All other virtues, like the plantain tree,
> Produce their fruit, but then their force is spent.
> Alone the marvelous tree of bodhicitta
> Will bear its fruit and grow unceasingly.

6. *Wrong-doing and obstructions are swiftly purified.* Even grave actions which would otherwise definitely bring intense suffering are purified by the altruistic intention. To purify their seeds as well, the ultimate altruistic intention is needed, namely the understanding of emptiness supported by the intention to become enlightened for the sake of all living beings. Even if we can sustain such thoughts for only a few moments, it is well worthwhile.

Asanga purified the obstructions which had prevented him from seeing Maitreya during twelve years of intensive practice when he was moved by pity for a bitch lying by the wayside, who was scratching an open wound on her hindquarters that was infested by maggots.[19]

In his *Way of the Bodhisattva* Shantideva says:

> As though they pass through perils guarded by a hero,
> Even those weighed down with dreadful wickedness

Will instantly be freed through having bodhicitta.
Who then would not place his trust in it?

These days there is a danger that people think intensive practice of only one aspect of the Buddha's teaching is more important and powerful than a good general understanding of the whole. His Holiness the Dalai Lama reiterates that recitation and prayers are a part of Buddhist practice, but that the most important feature of Buddhism is training ourselves to get rid of negative mental activity, to enhance positive states of mind and to develop those positive qualities which we do not yet possess. From his own personal experience he points out that love and compassion may be aroused by thinking about others' kindness to us. Yet there can still be an element of bias involved, since we may feel such love and compassion only towards those we consider friends. However, if we consider that all living beings, both friends and enemies, are the same in wanting happiness and not wanting suffering, the love and compassion that arise through these thoughts will be unbiased. This is precious advice.

7. *One's temporary and ultimate purposes will be accomplished effortlessly.* These purposes have to do with alleviating others' suffering and bringing them happiness by performing four kinds of activity—peaceful, increasing, powerful and fierce—which become easy to accomplish through the altruistic intention. It is the best way to remove obstacles and pacify sickness.

Once when the Brahmaputra had left its course and was about to flood Lhasa, a practitioner called Monlam Pelwa incised the following words on a stone: "If it is true that I am the Bodhisattva Monlam Pelwa,[20] then by the power of this truth may the flood recede," and it did. From then on monks would go to that spot during the great prayer festival held just after the lunar new year[21] and add stones which eventually formed a great rampart.

8. No harm or obstacles can affect one. A universal monarch is protected day and night by the kings of the four directions,[22] but the altruistic intention affords us twenty-four-hour protection of the very best kind. Once we think and act for others' benefit, we stop experiencing the results of our own selfish thoughts and actions, the cause of everything unwanted that we encounter.

The attainment of freedom from cyclic existence, from the pervasive suffering of conditioning, does not completely fulfill our own potential and limits the extent to which we can help others. Only enlightenment allows us to do both in the fullest way. Enlightenment is the result of Bodhisattva activities, which depend on the altruistic intention. To develop this supremely kindhearted intention we must awaken our Mahayana disposition. This depends upon establishing a relationship with a properly qualified spiritual teacher, who should possess the altruistic intention and the living lineage of instruction on how to develop it. It is said to be impossible to develop the altruistic intention without forming such a relationship.

We all have this latent disposition—the mind's potential to be free from all faults. Our present mental stains are not an integral part of us, for the mind's nature is clear light.[23] Intimately connected with this potential is the fundamental nature of the mind, its emptiness of inherent existence.

The reason only some people become enlightened while most do not is that not everyone is a proper vessel for the teachings, though each of us can become one. If the altruistic intention is the seed for enlightenment and the spiritual teacher the sower of that seed in the field of our mind, our responsibility is to cultivate the field to allow the seed to sprout and grow. The relationship with a spiritual teacher is part of this process and must be cultivated with body, speech and mind, as illustrated in the *Eight Thousand Verse Perfection of Wisdom Sutra*[24] by the Bodhisattva Sadaprarudita's[25] devotion to his spiritual teacher Dharmodgata and by Sudhana[26] in the *Gandavyuha Sutra*.

The Buddha Shakyamuni is praised as the white lotus among the thousand flower-like Buddhas of the fortunate era because he chose to come to our world during a time of degeneration when living beings are particularly obdurate. This choice was directed by his intense compassion and altruism.

There were many great scholars whom the Tibetans could have invited to Tibet, but despite immense hardships they persevered in trying to persuade Atisha to come because it was well known that he had developed the altruistic intention. In the end their perseverance bore fruit, the effects of which are still felt to this day. Although Atisha had more than one hundred and fifty spiritual teachers, to all of whom he was devoted, he always appeared particularly moved when the name of Dharmakirti of the Golden Isles was mentioned. When asked why this was so, he replied that any kindheartedness he had was due to this great master.

It is said that if we can develop the altruistic intention and the understanding of emptiness, namely that nothing has even a particle of inherent existence, we are in possession of "space-like" good qualities. Emptiness is present wherever there is space, and the understanding of emptiness extends to encompass all instances of it and thus is space-like. Wherever there is space there are living beings, and the altruistic intention is space-like in encompassing them all.

9. One will quickly develop the stages and paths of insight. Shantideva says that those who have both the aspiring and engaged altruistic intention constantly create huge stores of positive energy. Everything they do adds to it.

> A great and unremitting stream,
> A strength of wholesome merit,
> Even during sleep and inattention,
> Rises equal to the vastness of the sky.

This makes the rapid development of insights inevitable, since positive energy is the basic prerequisite for spiritual growth. In his *Yogic Deeds of Bodhisattvas*[27] Aryadeva points out that even when Bodhisattvas perform actions which in others would be negative, they create strong positive energy, so there is no need to mention the effect of their virtuous actions.

> In Bodhisattvas, through their intention,
> All actions, virtuous and non-virtuous,
> Become perfect virtue because
> They are in control of their minds.

Our approach to the altruistic intention, which is in fact the supreme expression of kindheartedness, is often distorted. Either we think of it as an exalted attitude which is far beyond our reach, or we are determined to practice only the highest and fastest means to enlightenment and regard the altruistic intention as a minor detail. But our spaceship may end up in the wrong place if we aren't careful. Our practice must be fuelled by the wish to emerge from cyclic existence, by the altruistic intention and by a correct understanding of reality, otherwise it will just be a simulacrum and not the real thing.

10. One becomes a source of all well-being and happiness. The Buddha's teachings are the root of happiness. They come from an enlightened being who is the outcome of many lives lived as a Bodhisattva. A Bodhisattva is born from the altruistic intention. There is no doubt that kindness is the key to happiness. In wishing others well and trying to help them we become happy ourselves. If we harbor harmful thoughts and express them, we hurt others and indirectly hurt ourselves.

In brief, developing the altruistic intention brings temporary and ultimate benefits in the form of good rebirths and enlightenment. It stops bad rebirths by purifying previous negativity and by preventing new negative actions. It insures good rebirths by enhancing previously created virtue and making freshly created virtue more powerful and inexhaustible. The ultimate form of "high status," the state of Buddhahood with all its adjuncts, is its result.

To gain enlightenment we must create the two great stores of insight and positive energy. Understanding reality creates the store of insight, but in order to rid ourselves of both the obstructions to liberation and to knowledge of all phenomena the vast store of positive energy created by the altruistic intention is essential.

Are we really interested in a good rebirth and enlightenment? Unless we are, there is a real danger that instead of being inspired by the benefits of the altruistic intention, we may just feel bored. We find it difficult to imagine anyone who is totally unselfish and only concerned with helping others. Our preoccupation with a good rebirth and enlightenment has to grow as strong as our interest in a long cool drink on a sweltering summer's day. Only when we are motivated by a real thirst for enlightenment will we be able to appreciate the advantages of developing the altruistic intention. The practices of the initial and intermediate levels are done to create a strong aspiration for high rebirth and liberation.

Faith is an essential foundation for developing the altruistic intention. We shouldn't think of faith as an unimportant preliminary. It extends from faith in the spiritual teacher to conviction in the necessity of all the paths of insight. In his *Precious Garland* Nagarjuna divides these paths into those which yield high status and those which yield definite goodness.[28] The basis for the former is the faith of conviction. The basis for the latter is wisdom. An excellent body, resources, companions and activity are what constitute high status. But high status is not restricted to a good rebirth within cyclic existence. The form bodies of an enlightened being[29] are supreme high status, resulting from the great store of positive energy created by practice of the first four perfections.[30] The wisdom body of an enlightened being is the ultimate form of definite goodness, resulting from the great store of insight created by practice of the last two perfections. All this is the final outcome of faith which enables us to develop qualities not yet developed and prevents those we already have from degenerating, while also strengthening them. Just as a burnt seed cannot produce a seedling, without faith there can be no growth of good qualities.

Contemplation of the advantages of the altruistic intention is meant to arouse faith and interest in it and in the practices of the Great Vehicle. Where there is faith, aspiration naturally follows and this leads to effort. Faith in the teachings leads to faith in the Buddha as their source and in the spiritual community who provide an example of how to practice them.[31]

Chapter 2
How to Develop the Altruistic Intention

There are four factors, four causes and four powers which can give rise to the altruistic intention. The four factors describe circumstances through which the altruistic intention may arise. In the first case the intention to become enlightened for the sake of all living beings results from experiencing or hearing reports of miraculous deeds by enlightened beings and Bodhisattvas.

In the second case, even though one has not had any direct experience of their marvelous deeds, studying the three categories of teaching[1] fills one with faith in enlightened beings and Bodhisattvas and, with a strong wish to emulate them, one develops the altruistic intention.

In the third case, fearing that the Mahayana teachings are declining and will vanish from this world and seeing that they play a unique part in removing the suffering of living beings and bringing them happiness, one wishes to prolong their presence and develops the altruistic intention to this end.

Finally, realizing that people are dominated by confusion as well as by a lack of self-respect and decency, and seeing that it is rare for anyone to aspire even to the liberation of a Hearer or Solitary Realizer, let alone to peerless enlightenment, one develops the altruistic intention to set an example and to encourage others to engage in the practices of the Great Vehicle.

Of the four causes that can give rise to the altruistic intention the first is one's excellent lineage or disposition. This refers to a strong interest in practicing the extensive and profound paths of the Great Vehicle and in attaining complete enlightenment. Relying on a properly qualified spiritual teacher is the second cause through which the altruistic intention may arise. The third possible cause for its arising is compassion and the fourth is a lack of discouragement by the hardships of cyclic existence.

If we are discouraged by the hardships of cyclic existence, we will not have the tenacity and energy to help other living beings. This requires the courage which comes from intense compassion. For such compassion to develop, we must cultivate a relationship with a properly qualified spiritual teacher, receive the essential instructions and put them into practice. The development of great compassion marks the awakening of our Mahayana disposition.

There are four forces through which the altruistic intention can arise. The first is the force of one's own extensive thought and initiative. The second is the force of others' inspiration and encouragement. The third is the force of causes formed by prolonged familiarity with the altruistic intention in previous lives and finally there is the force of applying the instructions on how to develop the altruistic intention that one has received from a spiritual teacher. It is said that the altruistic intention which is produced by the first and third forces is more reliable and stable than that arising from the other two.

If the enlightened ones and our spiritual teachers were to say what can help us most, they would indubitably indicate the altruistic intention. To develop it we must cultivate a sincere and close relationship with a spiritual teacher who possesses it. Through this we will create much positive energy and, hopefully, at least a little of our teacher's altruism and kindness will rub off on us. We should receive instructions, think deeply about them and practice till the seedling of the altruistic intention emerges. By nurturing it patiently, it will eventually become spontaneous and automatic, influencing all our actions in such a way that they become a constant expression of it.

Three obstacles prevent us from developing the altruistic intention. The first is our preoccupation with and clinging to the things of this life. To counteract it we must meditate on impermanence. The second is our clinging to the marvels of cyclic existence, which prevents our liberation. It is a contradiction to pray for liberation while longing for these things. To counteract this obstacle, we must think about the breadth and depth of this ocean of cyclic existence and how everything associated with it is a product of our misconceptions and a source of misery. Anything based upon our fundamental misconception of the self and on the disturbing emotions which arise from it is necessarily flawed, subject to decline and fraught with problems. The third obstacle is the idea that pacification of suffering and its causes, namely personal peace, is sufficient. This prevents us from developing the altruistic intention and from working for others in the most complete way. To counteract it we should take the altruistic intention to mind in a seed-like form. This means that before undertaking any practice or positive action, we make a concerted effort again and again to arouse clearly the wish to become enlightened for all living beings.

Compassion is the root of everything good. It is not just a transient feeling of empathy or pity but a stable emotion which is the outcome of learning to see all living beings as our mothers, of recognizing their kindness, feeling gratitude and developing the ability to regard them all as lovable. Compassion means that the suffering of others is as unbearable to us as being pierced by a sharp weapon. This emotion is strong enough to arouse the special wish to take personal responsibility for relieving the suffering of others and bringing them happiness.

There are two approaches to developing the altruistic intention. The seven cause and effect instructions have come down to us from the great Indian masters Asanga, Chandrakirti,[2] Chandragomin and Kamalashila.[3] The instructions for equalizing and exchanging self and others come from Shantideva. The Indonesian master Dharmakirti held both traditions and passed these on to Atisha. The old Kadampa masters taught the seven cause and effect instructions widely, while the tradition coming from Shantideva was somewhat less well known at that time. The new Kadampa masters, beginning with Je Tsongkhapa, placed equal emphasis on both techniques and taught how they could be combined. The two techniques are explained separately but are combined in practice.

THE SEVEN CAUSE AND EFFECT INSTRUCTIONS

Based upon boundless equanimity, we begin by seeing all beings as our mothers, recognizing their kindness, wishing to repay their kindness, seeing them all as lovable, arousing compassion, developing the special wish and from this generating the altruistic intention. The first six act as causes for the altruistic intention.[4] However, each step in the sequence is also a result of the preceding one.

The altruistic intention to attain enlightenment for all living beings will never arise without the special wish to shoulder responsibility for alleviating the suffering of living beings and bringing them happiness. This wish will only arise from unbiased, unprejudiced compassion that extends to every single living being. Compassion is not just necessary for developing the altruistic intention. It is the life-blood of the Great Vehicle.

At present we are moved by and wish to alleviate the suffering of those we consider our friends. Why is this? Because we feel close to them and see them as lovable. The closer we feel to them, the more lovable we consider them and the more unbearable even their smallest suffering seems to us. In the case of those we consider our enemies, not only do we feel unmoved by their suffering, we may wish it to continue for as long as possible. This is because we dislike them, do not feel close to them and do not see them as lovable. Then there are those who in our eyes are neither friends nor foes. We don't care if they suffer and we remain indifferent because we do not hold them dear. Unless we feel that all living beings are connected to us and are near, dear and lovable, unbiased compassion for them cannot arise.

The first three meditations—seeing all beings as our mothers, remembering their kindness and developing gratitude that wants to repay their kindness—are done to establish this sense of closeness and connection with all living beings. If they are done continuously in the proper way, the ability to see all living beings as lovable arises automatically without further effort. How much happier we would be if we could see all beings in this way! We wouldn't regard anyone as an enemy. There are many good reasons why we are, in fact, closely connected to all beings. Moreover, they are all pure by nature and what we find unattractive about them are temporary flaws. The proof of this is that when effective antidotes are applied, these unappealing aspects, such as the disturbing emotions, can be overcome.

The instructions for equalizing and exchanging self and others can also be used to develop the ability to see all living beings as lovable.[5] By concentrating on the faults of selfishness and the great benefits of cherishing others, by recognizing our dependence on other living beings, we can come to see them as wish-fulfilling jewels, the direct and indirect source of all our happiness. This then leads to the affection which regards all living beings as lovable, to compassion and the special wish, the three prerequisites for developing the altruistic intention. In a praise to the Buddha, Ashvagosha asks:

> Should I pay homage to you
> Or to the great compassion,
> Which makes you remain so long
> In cyclic existence, though you know its faults?[6]

At the beginning of his *Supplement to the Middle Way*[7] Chandrakirti, as it were, answers this question:

> Compassion alone is seen as the seed
> Of a Victor's rich harvest,
> As water for its growth, and as its ripening
> Into a lasting source of usefulness.
> And so, first, I pay homage to compassion.

It is essential at the beginning because without sufficient compassion we will not feel impelled to take responsibility for others' well-being, which is integral to Mahayana practice. Intermediately compassion remains essential, for without it we would easily become discouraged when we consider how many beings need our help, their unruly behavior, the difficult tasks that must be undertaken for their sake, the apparent endlessness of this work and the time frame in which it will take place. Strong compassion alone will protect us from self-concern and discouragement which might make us choose instead the way that leads to personal liberation. At the end it is compassion for all living beings that prevents an enlightened person from remaining in the state of solitary peace and bliss enjoyed by Hearer and Solitary Realizer Foe Destroyers. Compassion gives the impetus to use our own enlightenment to benefit living beings. From this we can see how precious and praiseworthy compassion is.

In the seven-part process certain steps give rise to compassion while others are the result of compassion. Compassion is central. Even a little more compassion would make an appreciable difference to all of us, including the smallest insects, and to our environment. It is the mainstay and root of the Great Vehicle. When we lose compassion and affection for one another, we also lose trust and as a result live in constant fear. Only if we truly want to develop compassion will we search for the means to do so. We like to hear about it and feel inspired, which is of course a good thing, but how rare it is for anyone to pursue the cultivation of compassion wholeheartedly with energy and enthusiasm. Many people recognize that compassion is the necessary basis for world peace. Every day we see, hear and read about the dreadful conflicts in different parts of our planet. We want our society to be more compassionate and we are looking for an instant and easy way to develop compassion, but such a method doesn't exist.

When we are able to see all beings as near, dear and lovable, we will find their suffering unbearable and will want to relieve it. This is compassion. In his *Great Exposition of the Stages of the Path* Je Tsongkhapa quotes the *Sutra Requested by Ocean of Intelligence*[8] to illustrate the difference between the compassion developed by practitioners of the Lesser and Greater Vehicles. A merchant had a beloved son who was obedient and pleasing to him in every way. One day this little boy was dancing around just by a cesspit when he suddenly fell in. His mother and aunts, who were nearby, saw what had happened and cried out in horror. They called for help but none of them got into the cesspit to rescue the child. Hearing the noise, the father came to see what had happened. As soon as he caught sight of his beloved son struggling in the stinking cess, he jumped right in to save his child without a second thought. The three realms[9] are the cesspit. The living beings are beloved children. The mother and aunts are the Hearers and Solitary Realizers. The father is the Bodhisattva who is impelled to act by the strength of his compassion.

We may become willing to accept personal responsibility for others, but are we capable of alleviating their suffering and giving them happiness? No one except an enlightened being has the capacity to help others in the fullest and most effective way. Thus it is imperative to attain complete enlightenment.

EQUANIMITY

Just as a fresco will only turn out well if it is painted on a smooth surface, equanimity is the essential foundation for the other insights. At present the affection we have for friends and loved ones is mixed with clinging attachment. Our aim is to develop an unbiased affection for all beings which is not tainted by such attachment. If a single being is excluded from this affection, what we do will not be a Mahayana practice. It is difficult for us even to think in this way, let alone embody it in our actions. Only Buddhas and Bodhisattvas possess this attitude. How worthwhile to try to arouse such thoughts and feelings for even a moment!

The first prerequisite, then, is the cultivation of boundless equanimity. Living beings are born again and again in cyclic existence because of their clinging attachment towards some and hostility towards others. Wouldn't it be wonderful if they could all remain in a state of equanimity? Why shouldn't they do so? May they do so! Thinking in this way is called the practice of boundless equanimity. However, more is required here, for we ourselves must learn to maintain a state of perfect equanimity free from attachment and aversion towards all beings. In his compilation of Pabongka Rinpoche's teachings on the stages of the path called *Liberation in the Palm of Your Hand* Kyabje Trijang Rinpoche[10] advises us to consider how all beings are exactly the same in their wish to avoid suffering and enjoy happiness. This being so, does it make sense to discriminate among them in our thoughts and actions?

At present we feel close to some and very distant from others. One way to develop equanimity is to begin by imagining someone who has neither helped nor harmed us in this life. We imagine their appearance and behavior as vividly as possible and watch what emotions arise. Probably there will be no strong emotions. Any attachment or aversion that is present is relatively easy to stop where such a person is concerned. Having practiced in this way for some time, we begin to work with friends, then with enemies and gradually extend the focus to include more and more living beings.

It is inadvisable to begin with an amorphous mass of living beings because the good feelings arising towards them en masse may be difficult to sustain in the case of individuals. Seeing a great assembly of monks can be inspiring but when we begin to look at individuals, whom we recognize and whose behavior may leave something to be desired, or we notice that, in fact, some of them are sleeping, critical thoughts will arise. This illustration shows that it is better to begin by developing equanimity towards specific individuals.

Soon after my arrival in India, I was living with many other monks in Buxaduar[11] in West Bengal and we all used to assemble for daily prayers. A nun was in the habit of circumambulating the assembly of monks with her hands pressed together in respect. This respect was not aimed at us all but only at a select few, particularly at the reincarnation of Pabongka Rinpoche. If anyone obstructed her view, she would move her hands, still in the gesture of respect, indicating that they should get out of the way. We were all rather afraid of her because she would scold us if she saw anything that did not meet with her approval. This is an amusing example of bias. Once you start being selective and exclusive, things become complicated. Pabongka Rinpoche's reincarnation died at the age of twenty-five, soon after taking his Geshe examination during which there were many remarkable signs visible to everyone. He had made brilliant progress in his studies and had won everyone's admiration.

The Victorious Ones and their spiritual children, the Bodhisattvas, do not get angry, no matter what physical or mental harm is inflicted on them. They are not tempted to retaliate but practice patience, thereby creating great virtue. Shantideva pays homage to all who possess that precious and excellent state of mind, the altruistic intention:

By contrast, good and virtuous thoughts
Will yield abundant fruits in greater measure.
Even in adversity, the Bodhisattvas
Never bring forth evil—
Only an increasing stream of goodness.

When Atisha was trying to decide what would be of greatest benefit to himself and others, he received many signs and predictions from spiritual teachers and meditational deities which indicated that he should dedicate himself to developing the altruistic intention. This is why he undertook the long and dangerous thirteen-month journey to Indonesia to study with Dharmakirti of the Golden Isles.[12] Having made fabulous offerings to this master, he requested complete instruction on how to develop the altruistic intention.

The master demanded to know whether he had the capacity to develop love and compassion and whether he was willing to remain with him for twelve years. Atisha replied that he thought he had that capacity and that he was willing to stay. And so he remained close to this master and it is said that their pillows touched at night.

Dharmakirti of the Golden Isles instructed Atisha fully on how to develop the altruistic intention and this transmission was like the complete contents of one pot being poured into another. Atisha at once began putting the instructions he received into practice and eventually developed the altruistic intention in such a powerful way that his teacher was truly satisfied and delighted. It is said that Atisha developed the altruistic intention primarily through the practice of equalizing and exchanging self and others.

To signify that he would be a great lord of the teachings, Dharmakirti of the Golden Isles gave Atisha a treasured copper and gilt statue of the Buddha Shakyamuni and predicted that he would propagate the teachings in a snowy land. In this way the auspicious connections were already established long before Atisha journeyed to Tibet. The fact that we still have access to Atisha's teachings is due to those who have treasured them through the centuries and to our own good actions in the past.

Without equanimity any love and compassion we develop will be partial, biased and tainted by clinging attachment. Attachment and aversion are major obstacles which the cultivation of equanimity can remove. Without these disturbing emotions we would experience peace and harmony, but we dislike to hear of stopping desire and all the emotions associated with it because it is pleasurable when these emotions first arise. Stealthily they masquerade as friends. They exaggerate the attractiveness of the object on which they focus, making us reach out for something non-existent which we can never possess. This brings frustration. Instead of getting what we want, we get much that we don't want. The pain and anger we feel destroy us, others and our whole environment.

What should we do about these emotions? Repressing them is pointless and though it may be useful to suppress them temporarily by distracting ourselves, they will simply return later. We need to apply antidotes so that disturbing emotions which have already arisen stop and those which have not yet arisen don't get the chance to begin. Normally meditation on ugliness is the main antidote to desire and meditation on love the main antidote to anger. Our aim in applying the correct antidotes continuously is no longer to respond with attachment and anger no matter what the provocation may be. Instead, like the Buddhas and Bodhisattvas Shantideva mentions, we learn to respond with non-attachment, non-aversion and with love and compassion.

Once we have succeeded in maintaining equanimity towards a neutral person, Je Tsongkhapa's *Great Exposition of the Stages of the Path* tells us to imagine someone to whom we feel near, who has helped and been kind to us and whom we find attractive and appealing. As we try to cultivate equanimity towards this person, we remember their good qualities. It is natural to feel attachment but we must try to curb it. When we are able to think of such a person with equanimity, we begin to work with the image of someone we dislike. This is the real challenge. As we think of the harm they have done us, how they have injured our friends or supported our enemies, and when we remember their horrible behavior, we automatically bristle with hostility.

How can we stop the attachment and hostility which arise spontaneously? Our notion of permanence is so strong that we see friends and enemies forever fixed in these roles, but in fact we constantly experience how unstable everything is. Our relationships are continuously in flux. When we are fully aware of their impermanent nature, our disturbing emotions will not be nearly so strong.

In his *Great Exposition of the Stages of the Path* Je Tsongkhapa quotes the *Sutra Requested by Excellent Woman Moon*,[13] "I have killed you all in the past and you have hacked and cut me too. We have all been enemies and killed each other. How can these thoughts of desire and attachment arise in you?"

From one life to the next our roles as friends and enemies change. But even in this life people who begin as friends may later in life become bitter enemies and vice versa. People who are friends in the morning may be foes by nightfall or the reverse. Someone you are talking to one moment may become your enemy in the next because of a single word, look or gesture. We have all seen these things happen.

Other great masters recommend that instead of trying to develop equanimity towards the neutral person, the friend and enemy one after the other, we should begin by imagining all three of them at once and by observing the different emotions that arise in relation to each. Why do we feel happy focusing on the friend? Because he or she has given us some help in this life or has done what we wanted. Why do we feel uncomfortable focusing on the enemy? Because he or she has harmed us in this life or acted in a way contrary to our wishes. Why do we feel indifferent towards the neutral person? Because he or she has neither helped nor harmed us.

Next we should think that this so-called friend has harmed and killed us in many other lives. The so-called enemy has been our father, mother, dearest friend, lover, beloved child and so on in other lives, while the neutral person is not really neutral because he or she has been both our closest friend and bitterest enemy in the past. To whom should we be attached, to whom hostile, since all have been both friends and foes at different times?

Assenting to the illusion of permanence, we cling to the friend and turn our back on the enemy. But our emotions, their behavior and our relationship with them are constantly changing and are unstable and unreliable. Therefore it makes sense to develop equanimity towards them.

If we consider their situation, we find that all living beings are the same in desiring happiness and wanting to avoid suffering. Considering our own situation, we may like some more than others but all of them have helped and supported us in the past. We may argue that certain people have not been at all helpful to us in this life but, in fact, all living beings have both helped and harmed us at different times. Our friends have been harmful in the past, our enemies helpful.

If we can develop equanimity towards the friend, the enemy and the neutral person, it becomes easy to extend it to other living beings. Equanimity stops our tendency constantly to judge and discriminate which leads to harmful emotions and actions. In the middle part of the *Stages of Meditation*[14] Kamalashila stresses the importance of gaining the ability to see all living beings as lovable—as lovable as a cherished child. Je Tsongkhapa, explaining this quotation in his *Great Exposition of the Stages of the Path*, says that before we can hope to see all living beings in this way, we must level the present unevenness created in our minds by attachment and aversion through equanimity.

Chapter 3
Cultivating Loving Affection

A field that is to be cultivated must be cleared of stones and weeds. It must be ploughed and prepared for the seed, if the crop is to grow well. By applying counteractions to the disturbing emotions, we prepare the field of the mind. If the seed of compassion is planted in a well-ploughed and irrigated field, it will grow easily. The ability to see all living beings as lovable will make it impossible to bear their suffering. This is the measure of compassion entirely free from prejudice, namely from closeness to some and distance from others. Loving affection for living beings is the water with which to irrigate the field of the mind and make it fertile.

But first we must build an irrigation system to bring in the water. This is done through seeing all beings as mothers, remembering their kindness and wanting to repay their kindness. Do we want to bring the water of loving affection into our field? What is our field like at present? Is it rough and stony, full of weeds and rubbish? If one year the crops fail, it is a disaster and people are very upset, but are we concerned about the field of our mind? Do we cultivate or neglect it? Do we sow the seed for a crop of extensive and profound insights? Do we irrigate the field and nurture new shoots? Do we feel it is a disaster if insights don't grow?

Many approaches for developing equanimity are described. It isn't necessary to employ all of them but only those which we find meaningful and helpful. The important thing is to overcome the disturbing emotions. Intense desire or anger give us no rest, no matter how comfortable our bed is. Attachment and hostility are like a chronic disease which never allows us to feel well. We are so used to these emotions that we hardly notice the discomfort they cause. But when they stop for even a short time, we experience an enormous sense of relief and tranquillity.

The idea of interdependence and selflessness can help us to develop equanimity, since concepts like "friend" and "foe" are mutually dependent. Friends and enemies do not exist as such from their own side but are imputed by thought. When contemplating the sameness of self and others, we do so from the conventional and ultimate points of view. Though we all appear different in many ways, we and others are exactly alike in that at a fundamental level we are empty of inherent existence.

What we are trying to develop is an attitude intent on others' well-being.[1] These others include all living beings, down to the smallest insect. Their well-being is happiness, of which the ultimate form is the state of enlightenment free from all suffering. Thus compassion which wishes to alleviate others' suffering, love which wishes to give them happiness, and the special wish by which we take responsibility for doing everything we can for them are attitudes dedicated to the well-being of others. It is quite impossible to develop such attitudes without affection for all living beings.

Loving affection is developed through the first three steps: recognizing all beings as our mothers, remembering their kindness, and out of gratitude wanting to repay that kindness. Kamalashila stipulates that we cannot cultivate these three without first developing a sense of equanimity. This cannot be done unless we contemplate the lack of certainty regarding friends and enemies, which is a practice of the intermediate level. However, we will only understand the instability of these relationships if we have thoroughly reflected on the connection between actions and their effects, a practice belonging to the initial level. This will help us to recognize the transience of relationships, since both we and others are controlled by our previous actions. Though someone may intend to be a friend, through the force of past actions they may instead become our enemy or vice versa.

The connection between actions and their effects cannot be proved by reasoning, and in order to gain conviction we need to think deeply about the Buddha's teaching. We will be prepared to do this only if we accept the validity of the Buddha and his teaching. Trust is implicit in taking refuge, but we will not seek protection from the depths of our heart unless we are afraid of the bad states of rebirth and of cyclic existence in general and have conviction that the Three Jewels can help us.

Such fear won't arise unless we meditate on our own impermanence, for this makes us think about what kind of rebirth awaits us. Meditating on impermanence cannot make an impact until we recognize the preciousness of our present human life. To appreciate this and to practice all these meditations in an effective way we need to cultivate a relationship with a properly qualified spiritual teacher who can guide us. This relationship becomes possible only if we purify ourselves and create positive energy.

When we understand how all these practices are interconnected, it is apparent why concentrating on one is not sufficient. In his expositions of the stages of the path Je Tsongkhapa provides us with all the practices we need in an easily accessible form—just like quick food, ready to eat and drink. That shouldn't make us undervalue the importance of these texts or think them simple, for they contain many lifetimes' worth of practices. In Tibet these texts were taught by some of the greatest masters.

RECOGNIZING BEINGS AS OUR MOTHERS

To enable affection for living beings to flow into our mind, we begin by trying to recognize all living beings as our mothers. This means we think about the closest of all relationships, that of mother and child. Sutra says that we cannot state with certainty that we have never been born in this particular country, in this particular place as this particular kind of being. Moreover, we cannot state with certainty that a particular creature has never been our mother. Since neither cyclic existence nor living beings have any demonstrable beginning, none of us can find a beginning to the rebirths we have taken. So how could we claim that we have never been in the womb of a particular being? When we think about this for some time, the idea that all living beings have been our mother will arise. However, the great masters say that this train of thought alone will not induce a strong sense of conviction.

These masters recommend that we begin by imagining our mother of this life before us, evoking her presence—her appearance and behavior—as vividly as possible. Whether at this point we like her or not, we don't need to prove to ourselves that she is our mother because we know it. Then we should think that she has also been our mother many times in the past. To support this line of thinking we take as example the Buddha's accounts of how his own mother had mothered him many times in previous existences. Of course, this demands confidence in the Buddha's statements and in the existence of past and future lives.

Having thought about how she has been our mother many times in the past, we then begin to think about how all other living beings have also been our mothers. We have had countless lives in which we have had mothers, more lives than there are living beings. Thus, in fact, all living beings have been our mothers not just once but many times, and they have even been our mothers many times in human existences. In this sequence we move from the specific to the general, which is considered the most effective order to follow.

We conceive of ourselves in terms of body and mind. Thinking about the mind, we can trace how today's consciousness is a continuity of yesterday's and how the consciousness of this present period of our life is the continuity of our consciousness as a child. Our consciousness at the moment when we emerged from the womb was a continuity of consciousness while in the womb. Consciousness at the moment of conception must have been preceded by a moment of consciousness, since from the Buddhist point of view mind can only come from mind. It cannot come from anything material composed of the four elements, as those who do not accept the existence of past and future lives would probably assert. Thus, consciousness at the moment of conception is a continuity of that in the intermediate state, which in turn is preceded by consciousness at the moment of death.

When we look at how a moment of, for instance, visual perception of yellow arises, we discover the presence of various causes: the objective condition, something yellow; the main condition, the eye sense faculty; and the immediately preceding condition, a previous moment of awareness.[2] Thus awareness is always preceded by awareness though the kind of awareness which is operative is not always the same. While we are in very deep sleep, the most subtle state of consciousness operates, which is similar to the consciousness present at the time of death. While dreaming, a slightly less subtle form of mental consciousness is active, which is comparable to the intermediate state. When we are awake, coarse states like the sense perceptions function, which are compared to rebirth. The kind of awareness present at conception is very subtle.

We can easily accept that today's awareness is a continuity of yesterday's because we can remember what happened yesterday. But we do not necessarily remember everything that happened yesterday! The basic hurdle here is belief in past and future lives. To develop conviction with regard to rebirth we turn to scriptural passages and use the reasoning described above. We should be prepared to contemplate this matter for a long time and not expect to gain conviction quickly or easily. It needs to be approached with an open mind and without bias in favor of our own current views. No one is forcing us to accept rebirth. Some believe in rebirth and have reasons to support their view; others do not. We should consider both arguments and make our own unbiased evaluation.

There are instances of quite ordinary people who have memories of a past life which can be substantiated, like the little Indian girl from a family of farmers in the Punjab who remembered where she had lived in her last life and how she had been killed in a bicycle accident. She kept talking about this until she persuaded her father to let her take him to that place, which she had never visited before in this life, and she was reunited with her previous parents who confirmed her story.

If she had a previous life, wouldn't it be strange to say that we haven't? If we have been around before but don't remember it, we can surmise that we will be taking birth again until we manage to rid ourselves of the causes which propel us involuntarily from one life into another. In this life happiness is of great concern to us but seen from this new perspective we will need happiness in those future lives too. If we are in doubt about rebirth, it seems better, safer and wiser to act as though it exists. If we don't and it does, we are in trouble.

For Tibetans the existence of past and future lives is a basic premise. Some people have gained logical conviction but for most it is just a natural assumption with which they have grown up. We see old Tibetan men and women in exile here in India circumambulating a temple or a library containing sacred books. Even during the monsoon when it is slippery, they come day after day, sheltering under their umbrellas. They are not doing it for the exercise but because they think that this is something worthwhile which will affect their future lives.

In Tibetan society old people never felt their lives were meaningless. Their children would tell them to take it easy, to let them get on with managing the household and not to worry about these things but to think good thoughts and do their practice—a gentle way of deflecting their interference but equally a sign of gratitude to their parents.

At home in my childhood the tsampa and cheese containers and tea in a clay pot were brought to our grandfather's or grandmother's bed, not on a clean shining breakfast tray, but this was all they needed. They had a string to pull the big family prayer wheel and their own small prayer wheel in their right hand and prayer beads in their left hand. We children ran in and out to drink some tea and eat a little tsampa. We vied with one another for the honor of sleeping with our grandmother. Old people never felt useless. I don't think we made a mistake living like that, even though society didn't make much "progress" and people spent their lives very much as their parents had done before them.

In his *Letter to a Friend* Nagarjuna says that if we think of our mother's mother and her mother and so on, the number of mothers is limitless.

> If you counted all your mothers
> With juniper berry-sized balls of earth,
> The earth would not be enough.

Kyabje Trijang Rinpoche suggests that instead of thinking of our mother and her mother and so forth, it is better to think of our mother in this life, our mother in the previous life, our mother in the life before that and so forth. The number of mothers we have had is limitless. We should think how our father of this life, our siblings, our friends and even our enemies have all been our mothers in the past. The insects around us have been our mothers. Eventually, if we succeed in doing this practice properly, we can look at any living being and think, "I was this creature's child. When it mothered me, it cherished me tenderly and tried to protect me from harm and give me happiness."

REMEMBERING AND REPAYING KINDNESS

When seeing all living beings as our mothers becomes as natural as recognizing our mother of this life, we think about the mother's kindness which is there in the beginning, in the middle and at the end. In the beginning, as soon as she realizes she is pregnant, our mother is careful about what she eats and how she moves. If she is sick, she immediately considers whether the prescribed medicines will affect her unborn child. Her body fluids nurture us. Without all this, we could not have survived in the womb and would not be alive today.

She suffers the pains of labor while giving birth to us. Yet when she sees us, she is delighted with the helpless little creature she has produced. She places us tenderly against her body to give us milk from her breasts. She touches us gently with her hands, holds us in her arms, looks at us lovingly, smiling, speaking sweet words to us, watching for the first trace of a smile on our face. Though modern drugs may make childbirth less painful, I wonder if the conditions under which many women deliver their babies these days are so much better. While we are babies, we are totally dependent on our mother for everything and cannot survive without her. A mother's whole attention is focused on her infant and its needs.

Although we may have other caretakers, our mother is the main one. When we are small we adore our mother and there is no place we would rather be than in her arms or on her lap. If something is wrong, we want to be picked up by her and not by anyone else. We cannot bear to be separated from her which makes it hard for her to do anything on her own. Her love for us is mixed with attachment. She would like us always to turn towards her as we did in our early childhood. But all too soon we become independent and that is when the trouble starts.

Our aim in cultivating the altruistic intention is to become kinder, less selfish people. That doesn't just mean developing peaceful physical and verbal behavior but becoming sensitive to the suffering and lack of happiness other living beings experience. This sensitivity then gives rise to compassion and love with a sense of personal responsibility for their well-being, which leads to the intention to become completely enlightened in order to be best able to help them. When this wish governs all we do, we have developed the altruistic intention and our actions become the extensive deeds of Bodhisattvas. Prayers and wishes are not enough because this does not come naturally. We have to work at it and train ourselves.

The purpose of trying to perceive all living beings as our mothers is to see them in the very closest role. Their kindness, both when they have been our mothers and when they haven't, is inestimable. They are truly like wish-fulfilling jewels, for everything we need and want comes through them. Despite this we blame them for everything which is wrong with our lives because we cannot bear to recognize the true culprit, our selfishness. The root of all the disturbing emotions which lead us to act negatively and the source of our suffering is our misconception of the self and our exaggerated self-concern. To counter these we must develop the two kinds of altruistic intention because unless we rid ourselves of this misconception and of our egoism we will never find the happiness we are seeking. Ideally we must banish them completely, but even if we cannot completely get rid of them for the time being, we can stop their pervasive influence.

All living beings are suffering. Some suffer more mentally, others more physically but all of us are afflicted by both kinds of suffering. Though some may look grander, really all are the same in this respect. We only need to get to know others a little more intimately to discover that they too are suffering. No one has forced suffering upon us as some kind of punishment. Our own disturbing emotions are to blame.

The problem is that we and our disturbing emotions seem totally inseparable. When the teachings tell us that the disturbing emotions are our enemy and we watch how they dominate us, the task of getting rid of them appears overwhelming and we can end up hating ourselves. Though these emotions seem to be an integral part of us, they are not. We can get rid of them and instead make positive emotions and attitudes such as love, compassion and the altruistic intention as much a part of ourselves as the disturbing emotions are now.

When everything we do is influenced by kindness and compassion, our actions will only bring benefit, and we will have become our own and others' protectors and sources of refuge. Since the nature of all living beings is pure and good, we have a natural propensity for the limitless development of these positive emotions. Every living being has Buddha-nature, the potential to become enlightened by overcoming all limitations and faults and developing extraordinary qualities. The fact that the nature of our mind is clear light means that the disturbing emotions are only a temporary manifestation which can be ended through the correct application of antidotes. We can develop the altruistic intention if we really want to. However, it is a contradiction to claim that we want to do this and at the same time to reject the idea of recognizing all living beings as our mothers because this acts as a foundation for the altruistic intention.

When we consider the kindness of our mother, we should remember how helpless we were. We couldn't stand, walk, speak, eat or control our bowels. None of this came naturally. She taught us to the best of her ability how to do all these things. She did it with patience and love and would rather have been sick herself than see us sick. Later she used the money which she had earned through her hard work and saved carefully to insure that we got a good education. Even though we probably considered it as interference, she continued to try to steer us in what she considered a good direction and was anxious that we should marry someone suitable. Not only has she done her best in this life to protect us from pain and suffering and give us happiness, but she did so in many other lives as well. She has been so preoccupied with it that she herself has often had no opportunity to improve her education or see to her own spiritual development. Her needs have taken second place, while those of her children have been more important. Surely she deserves our respect.

Our fathers, siblings, friends and enemies have all nurtured us like this in the past. Here we have focused on the behavior of human mothers but if we watch animals, we will see how they care for their young, how birds when they find a juicy worm take it straight back to their brood. What a difficult job they have finding sufficient food for their hungry fledglings!

The devotion of mothers to their young is illustrated by the following story. When King Srongtsen Gampo sent his minister to win the hand of the Chinese princess he wished to marry, there were many other suitors and one of the tests they had to perform was to pair fifty mares with their fifty grown foals, all of whom looked very similar. The other suitors failed but the Tibetan minister was very shrewd and decided to feed the mares hay. Each mare immediately began pushing some of her hay towards her own foal, making it clear which foals and mares were mother and child.

Actually the story goes that the Tibetan king was not as interested in the Chinese princess as in the statue of the Buddha Shakyamuni which she brought with her.[3] This is not intended to denigrate the princess in any way but the fact remains that the princess' life was short compared to the statue's. It is still in Lhasa and has held a place of honor in the lives of Tibetans for hundreds of years. Seeing this statue was the climax of their pilgrimages from distant places. If Tibetans had been interested in turning it into a financial asset they could have made a fortune by now, charging for tickets to see it, since it is visited by everyone who comes to Lhasa!

If we truly want to find freedom, we must simplify our life by overcoming our tendencies to be greedy and discontented. Instead we should become easy to please and satisfy. Although a simple life-style is generally lauded by all Buddhist schools of thought,[4] Vaibhashikas and Sautrantikas lay particular stress on it, since they see craving as one of the chief factors which bind us to cyclic existence. The cultivation of non-attachment is therefore of paramount importance to them because it is the precious disposition that acts as a basis for all higher insights.

Chittamatrins see the mind-basis-of-all[5] as the source for cyclic existence and the state beyond sorrow, and for them the naturally abiding disposition is the seed for developing an uncontaminated state of mind which is present in the mind-basis-of-all. For Madhyamikas the disposition is two-fold: the clear and cognizant nature of the mind is the developmental disposition which eventually becomes the wisdom body of an enlightened being. The emptiness of the mind is the innate disposition which will be the nature body of an enlightened being.[6] This means that all living creatures will eventually attain enlightenment and that it is just a question of time. The altruistic intention is the special cause of enlightenment. Since we have the capacity to develop it, why not begin now?

In his *Compendium of Training*[7] Shantideva uses the analogy of an old mother, blind and deranged without anyone to guide her, who stumbles to the edge of a dangerous cliff. If her child is nearby, in whom else would she place her hope and trust? Living beings, our very kind mothers, are blind because they don't know what is constructive and what is harmful. Both their aspirations and the actions they lead to are misguided. Since their ideas and actions are flawed, they make many mistakes, which is like stumbling to the edge of a cliff. They lack good counsel about what is and what is not worth doing. They are deranged by the three poisons and about to plunge into the abyss of bad rebirths. In comparison to them we are in a privileged position. We are human and have the ability to distinguish between benefit and harm. We have access to teachers who can explain what should be cultivated and discarded, and we can ride in the Great Vehicle. When we consider how much other living beings suffer and how they lack happiness, we will realize that the responsibility of helping these old mothers is ours. If we don't do anything to help, it shows our heartless ingratitude.

In his *Letter to a Disciple*[8] Chandragomin writes that these living beings, who are in fact extremely close to us, are submerged in the ocean of cyclic existence and it is as if they are drowning in the turbulent waves of birth, death and taking rebirth again, so that we do not recognize them. What could be worse than abandoning them and leaving them to their fate?

In his *Heart of the Middle Way* Bhavaviveka[9] says:

Moreover, previously I have been possessed
By the demon of disturbing emotions,
And like rubbing salt into a wound,
I have made those already in pain suffer.
What better way to show gratitude and repay
Those who in other lives have helped me
By giving love, and pleasing me with their service,
Than through helping them to reach
The state beyond sorrow?

Providing living beings with the food, clothes, friends, servants and other worldly things they need is a way of repaying their kindness and creates positive energy. However, in the past they have been under the protection of powerful kings and others who have provided for all their needs, but it never did them much good. They are still searching for happiness and are still overwhelmed by suffering. Despite all the worldly excellence they have enjoyed, ordinary living beings continue to experience the pervasive suffering of conditioning and endure pain of many kinds. Worldly opulence cannot cure the wound of their suffering in cyclic existence—indeed it is just like rubbing salt into the wound because these things bring only contaminated and fleeting happiness which is actually the suffering of change. The best way to repay their kindness is to help them gain lasting happiness, the state of highest enlightenment, free from all suffering, beyond both cyclic existence and solitary peace.

When the first three steps: recognizing all beings as our mothers, remembering their kindness and feeling the wish to repay their kindness are practiced properly, no effort needs to be made to cultivate the loving affection which sees all living beings as near and as dear as a beloved child, since this will arise quite spontaneously.

Chapter 4

Love and Compassion

When intense affection is present, we will respond with compassion and love to others' suffering and lack of happiness. In his *Great Exposition of the Stages of the Path* Je Tsongkhapa next explains how to cultivate love, while other masters explain the cultivation of compassion first. The order is not important. Affection which sees all living beings as near and dear is one form of love. The kind that is now cultivated is the willingness to give others happiness. Here love consists not only of thinking, "If only all living beings could be happy. May they be happy!" but also of, "May I be the one who helps them find happiness."

It is said that such love creates more merit than filling all world systems in the universe with offerings. In his *Precious Garland* Nagarjuna mentions eight benefits that come from feeling strong love for even just a moment:

> You will be loved by gods and humans
> And you will be protected by them.
> You will be happy and enjoy much pleasure
> And be unharmed by weapons or poison.
> You will effortlessly achieve your aims
> And be born in the realm of Brahma.

We will be loved by gods and humans because someone who is loving and peaceful is attractive to all, while an angry person or poisonous creatures like snakes and scorpions repulse others and fill them with fear. Because others will love us if we are loving, they will come to our rescue and protect us from obstacles. We will experience inner joy and happiness of other kinds. Even small acts of kindness lovingly performed give us joy and a sense of exhilaration.

We will be protected from poisonous weapons and harm because the peaceful ethos surrounding us will make our enemies vanish. In praise of the Buddha[1] Je Tsongkhapa says:

> Without arrows, weapons or armor,
> Alone you have defeated in battle
> Every one of millions of demons—
> Who but you knows how to do this?

He is speaking of the Buddha's love, which was his best protection. With love as strong as this it is possible to gain supreme enlightenment in one lifetime, but being even a little more kind and loving would bring us many benefits.

Atisha's master Shila Dharmarakshita[2] was a great practitioner of love and compassion, although he was a proponent of the Vaibhashika view which is a philosophical position normally associated with the Lesser Vehicle. Once there was a sick man living near this master, who had been told his illness could be cured if he got some flesh taken from a living person. The man was in despair because he thought this would be impossible to procure. When Dharmarakshita heard about it, he offered flesh from his own thigh. These days an injection might well have been all that was needed!

The man recovered and later when they met, Dharmarakshita asked him how he was. The man replied that he had fully recovered but that Dharmarakshita must have experienced terrible pain as a result of his sacrifice. Dharmarakshita replied that it was nothing, since one had to be prepared even to die for others.

In fact he had experienced dreadful pain and had been quite unable to sleep. When he finally did fall asleep near dawn, he dreamed a white figure came, spat on the wound and passed his hand over it, whereupon the wound at once healed. The figure praised him and told him that it was necessary to do difficult things like this if he really wished to attain enlightenment. When he awoke he found that there was no trace of the wound left. He had been miraculously healed and he realized that the white figure in his dream had been Chenrezig.[3]

The intensity of his compassion purified his karmic obstructions and he was able to understand reality. The meaning of Nagarjuna's six great works on reasoning[4] became clear to him without the need for a teacher's explanations and he began to recite these works as a daily practice. This shows us that love and compassion have the power to accomplish others' well-being, purify our obstructions and create great stores of merit.

Another of Atisha's masters, known as the "Practitioner of Love,"[5] lived in seclusion on the banks of the Ganges. He composed beautiful songs of experience about the practice of giving and taking, wishing that others' suffering and their three poisons might ripen on him and that they might experience his happiness. Maitreya appeared to him and praised the sweetness of his songs. If we want dreams and visions, why don't we try to strengthen our love and compassion?

In the development of love the great masters again encourage us to begin with a specific person and then extend the feeling to others. Great love and great compassion, which are directed towards all living beings, have three features from the point of view of their cause, their nature and their result: they are induced by the first three steps of seeing all beings as our mothers, remembering their kindness and wishing to repay their kindness. They are a strong and stable wish to alleviate the suffering of others and to give them happiness, sufficiently intense to yield the special wish. They produce the determination to accept responsibility for the well-being of others.

When cultivating love we imagine our mother of this life as vividly as possible and think how very little ordinary happiness she enjoys, not to mention uncontaminated happiness. The brief happiness she experiences is really only the suffering of change. The closer we feel the more unbearable her situation will appear and the more we will want her to find lasting happiness. While trying to develop love, we should say the words, "Wouldn't it be wonderful if she were happy! May she be happy! May I be the one who helps her to find happiness!" with feeling from the depths of our heart. Ideally our loving thoughts move us to say these words, but even if we are still unable to feel this way, saying the words again and again will eventually start to have a positive effect. When we can respond to our mother's lack of happiness with real love, we begin to think about others who are close to us, then about neutral people and finally about enemies.

Why should we want to help our enemies or to give them happiness? Here are various useful ideas to consider. One approach is to think that the harm they have done us is, in fact, the result of our own past negative actions through which we have set ourselves up as a target for their harm. We could also consider how those who harm us are totally driven by their disturbing emotions. If someone in our family, someone we love dearly, becomes insane and tries to harm us, we wouldn't think of taking revenge but would try to help them regain a normal state of mind. Living beings, our mothers, are crazed by their disturbing emotions. Those who harm us are in particular need of our love and compassion.

THE WISH TO REMOVE SUFFERING

When cultivating compassion we follow the same process, but instead of contemplating their lack of happiness, we think about the different kinds of suffering which afflict living beings. Then, beginning with our own mother, we wish them freedom from suffering and the causes of suffering. Again it is important to voice the wish and our resolve to be the one who helps. In *Liberation in the Palm of Your Hand* Kyabje Trijang Rinpoche writes that imagining a sheep which is about to be slaughtered can be a powerful way of arousing compassion. Think of the scene in the abattoir and of the slaughterer tying a rope round the sheep's neck. Then he ties the front legs and the back legs tightly together, making it absolutely impossible for the sheep to escape. The sheep realizes it is about to die and feels dreadful fear and suffering. All it can do is gaze mournfully at the face of its executioner.

We should imagine ourselves in the same position. We might think that a sheep doesn't really feel acute fear or suffering, but that isn't true. There isn't any difference between this sheep and the others grazing peacefully on the hillside. It's just a question of time till they face the same fate. And all of them have been our mothers. Then we should think, "Wouldn't it be wonderful if they were free from suffering! May they be free from suffering! May I be the one who helps free them from suffering!"

Some living beings are suffering outright physical or mental pain. All ordinary beings are afflicted by the suffering of change and the pervasive suffering of conditioning. Those in the hell realms suffer from extreme heat and cold. Those in the realm of hungry spirits experience intense hunger and thirst, while animals are afflicted by stupidity and fear. People who look as if everything is fine are constantly running after what is harmful, which insures their future suffering.

Strong compassion and love will induce the special wish to take personal responsibility for others. What is the difference between this wish and the wish to repay others' kindness? The *Great Exposition of the Stages of the Path* explains the difference through the example of a trader who is first considering a business deal and who then makes up his mind to go through with it.

But are we able to help living beings in the way we want? Often others' problems leave us feeling quite helpless. Despite their great realizations Hearers, Solitary Realizers and even Bodhisattvas cannot help living beings in the way a Buddha can. If we have practiced taking refuge in the proper way, we will know the superlative qualities enlightened beings possess—their physical, verbal and mental qualities, their compassion, knowledge, power and the kind of activities they can perform. Only by gaining complete enlightenment will we be able to help others in the fullest possible way. And thus the altruistic intention to become enlightened for the sake of others is born. It is at this point that accumulation of the great stores of positive energy and insight for three long aeons begins.

EXCHANGING SELF AND OTHERS

Although both the seven-part cause and effect practice and the equalizing and exchange of self and others give rise to the altruistic intention, the latter is said to produce a stronger form of it. In the cause and effect sequence we concentrate on the kindness of living beings while they have been our mothers, thereby focusing on past kindness. When using the latter approach, we consider the kindness of living beings at all times, not only as our mothers. We examine their kindness and our dependence on them in the past, present and future, which produces a stronger sense of how kind they have been. This practice is sometimes referred to as one to be kept secret from those who are not ready for it because it would simply overwhelm them. Speaking about the practice of exchanging self and others in his *Way of the Bodhisattva* Shantideva says:

> Those desiring speedily to be
> A refuge for themselves and other beings
> Should interchange the terms of "I" and "other,"
> And thus embrace a sacred mystery.

All the Buddha's teachings are about training the mind because they are intended to help us to develop good qualities and positive states of mind and to get rid of faults, especially all unpeaceful and disturbed states of mind. However, based on this teaching and on the practice of giving away our happiness and taking on the suffering of others, a special tradition of mental training developed.

Atisha, who held the lineage of teachings coming from Shantideva, brought them to Tibet where the Kadampa masters gave them only to a few selected students until the time of Geshe Chekawa, who wrote the *Seven Points of Training the Mind*.[6] The Kadampa masters described the method for developing the ultimate altruistic intention before describing how to develop the conventional altruistic intention. However, Shantideva and Je Tsongkhapa describe the latter first. In his *Great Exposition of the Stages of the Path* Je Tsongkhapa explains how to develop the ultimate altruistic intention in the context of training in the perfection of wisdom.

Geshe Chekawa's text begins with the advice to "train in the preliminaries." The preliminaries are none other than the practices of the initial and intermediate levels as described in the *Great Exposition of the Stages of the Path*. By thinking about suffering in the bad states of rebirth and in all states of cyclic existence in relation to ourselves, we build the foundation for understanding the suffering of others and feeling empathy towards them. This eventually gives rise to compassion.

Equalizing and exchanging self and others has five steps. The first is developing the ability to express in action the insight that we and others are the same. The second is to examine the faults of selfishness from many different angles. The third is to recognize the great benefits of cherishing others. The fourth is the actual practice of exchange. Finally to strengthen compassion and love, we take on the suffering of others and give away our happiness.

We and others are the same in that we all experience unwanted suffering and lack happiness. We all long for happiness and want to avoid suffering. We are also the same in lacking any kind of intrinsic existence. But how do we behave? We feel and act as though our own happiness were the only important thing in the world. All our efforts are directed to the pursuit of this happiness and to our attempts to avoid suffering. Now we should try at least to be equally concerned about others' happiness and the alleviation of their suffering. Even this first step is difficult to implement in thought and action.

An important place to begin is by thinking that, generally speaking, what we don't like and want is also disliked and unwanted by others. What we like and want they would enjoy as well. If we are really thirsty and it is hard to find clean water, do we just gulp down a whole glass without giving a thought to our equally thirsty companion? We can begin at this level by remembering and considering others' needs. Even such simple kinds of sharing are hard to practice. The aim is to devote as much energy to others' well-being as to our own.

Exchanging self and others is impossible unless we have repeatedly considered the faults of self-concern and the benefits of cherishing others. Although self-concern is bad, that doesn't mean that we are bad. The self and self-concern are not identical. Our nature is essentially pure and good, which is why we can become free from faults. We can also grow more familiar with and develop greater goodness and wisdom.

Can self-concern ever be positive? What about the wish for personal happiness and for liberation from cyclic existence? What if one remains in such a state of freedom? Is liking ourselves bad? Is self-concern only a fault from the Mahayana perspective? Then what about Shantideva's statement that self-concern is the cause of everything unwanted and troublesome in our lives? These are some of the questions we need to examine.

There are many degrees of self-concern. The real culprit is the feeling, "As long as I'm alright, as long as I'm happy, that's all that matters. I don't care about the others." And even worse is the willingness to manipulate and exploit others to insure our own happiness. Some people may protest that they lack self-concern because they hate themselves, but self-hatred stems from self-concern and a deep frustration at not being able to achieve what one wants for the self.

Shantideva points out that all our happiness comes from cherishing others and all our fears and misfortunes from cherishing the self:

> All the joy the world contains
> Has come from wishing happiness for others.
> All the misery the world contains
> Has come through wanting pleasure for oneself.

We have always been in search of personal happiness and have always tried to avoid suffering, but our quest has been unsuccessful. Enlightened beings behaved differently. They put the concerns of others first and forgot about themselves. This accounts for their success in finding supreme happiness. The great benefits of cherishing others and the disadvantages of selfishness are described to inspire us to make a change.

As mentioned before, there is the cultivation of "boundless equanimity," the wish for others to live in a state free from attachment and hostility. Then there is the equanimity which is free from bias and serves as a basis for the seven-part cause and effect process. Equanimity in the context of equalizing and exchanging self and others refers to seeing all living beings as just like ourselves and fostering the wish to help them all find happiness and alleviate their suffering, whether they are friends, enemies or those with whom we do not have any special relationship in this life.

Kyabje Trijang Rinpoche, in his text on training the mind,[7] suggests that we consider six points from a conventional perspective and three from the ultimate point of view in order to arouse this wish to benefit all equally.

Firstly, none of us wants to experience the slightest suffering, not even in our dreams. Our hunger for happiness is insatiable. This applies to every living being, even insects. On what grounds can we discriminate between them by helping some and ignoring others? It makes sense to help them all equally.

Secondly, if ten beggars come to our door and all are equally destitute, how can we discriminate between them? Living beings don't experience pure happiness—no need to mention that—but even ordinary happiness evades them and is as rare as stars during daylight. It makes sense to give them all happiness equally.

Thirdly, imagine there is an epidemic and ten people come to the doctor with the same disease. On what grounds would he choose to treat some and not the others? All living beings are dominated by the disturbing emotions, which are a sickness, and they experience the three kinds of suffering—the suffering of pain, of change and the pervasive suffering of conditioning. It makes sense to help alleviate their suffering equally.

We might agree with all of this but still wonder why we should take personal responsibility for their plight. But if we consider our relationship to them, the reason will be obvious. The fourth point is that if we are interested in achieving good rebirths and enlightenment, and as students of the Great Vehicle ostensibly we are, then we must realize that none of these aims can be accomplished except in relation to other living beings. Even the most ordinary forms of happiness we desire are impossible without others' cooperation. These others have been in the closest possible relationships to us in the past and have nurtured and protected us. How can we discriminate between them? It makes sense to cherish them all equally.

We often react to this by thinking that they have certainly also harmed us. The fifth point is that in all our different relationships with them, they have harmed us far fewer times than they have helped us. We need only look at the present. How many beings are harming us? How many are helping to support our life, whether intentionally or unintentionally? We owe our body, possessions, survival, well-being and happiness to them. Just think of the role cows and sheep play in our lives. The assistance we receive far outweighs the harm, so it makes sense to help them all equally in return.

The sixth point is that we are all going to die sooner or later. All living beings are in the jaws of death with no idea when those jaws will snap shut. If we discriminate, we are as absurd as a group of prisoners on death row, who start quarreling although they know they are to be executed in the morning. Instead of discriminating we should try to be kind and helpful to all.

The three points to consider from an ultimate perspective are that, firstly, we tend to see people fixed in their roles as friend or foe, whereas enlightened beings, who have rid themselves of all stains, see every living being as a kind mother. To someone enlightened a person on their left massaging them gently with aromatic oil and one on their right cutting them with a knife are equally near and dear. Our prejudices are meaningless.

Secondly, their roles as friends and foes are not definitive because relationships constantly change—friends become foes and foes become friends—making all our discrimination a waste of time. Thirdly, we may see a certain person as a friend but someone else will see the same person as a foe. Who is right? Friend and foe are terms designated in dependence on each other. Does the way we discriminate make sense?

Through personal instructions our spiritual teachers give us the pith of the teachings. Kyabje Trijang Rinpoche has drawn together these points from different texts, food for our spiritual nourishment! Are we willing to taste it?

We should try to observe our judgmental attitudes and how we react with attachment and hostility, the root of the many misfortunes we experience. These emotions are the jailors that keep us locked up in the prison of suffering. They are the butcher who leads us to the slaughterhouse. They are our chronic disease which produces countless symptoms and stops us sleeping peacefully at night.

Overcoming these disturbing emotions and at least "equalizing" self and others is the root of all temporary and ultimate happiness. It is the sole path which all Buddhas and Bodhisattvas follow and the quintessence of all practices. We must make up our mind that we and others are just the same and resolve to stop feeling close to some and distant from others. Though it takes quite a long time to talk or read about all of this, it is possible to think about it quite quickly. We should try to do this briefly every morning. Though it is not easy to put into practice, change will come if we persevere. To motivate ourselves we should think again and again that our self-centeredness is the source of all our misfortunes and our concern for others the source of all that is excellent.

We may wonder if it is really possible to exchange self and others. Our attitude to the body is an instructive example. Though the body is unclean, in many ways futile and lacking any intrinsic existence, we see it as clean, very important and objectively existent. These perceptions come naturally because of our great familiarity with them. Familiarity is the key to how we see things. It is possible for us to feel as personally involved in protecting others' bodies as we do in protecting our own. Once this happens, we will be able to do things for others without needing to boast about what we have done and without the hope for anything in return. After all, we eat to nourish our body without expecting anything in return.

We try to protect ourselves from even a single unpleasant word. Such an intense feeling of wanting to protect living beings from even the slightest harm depends on the cultivation of compassion. Many people are afraid to be in a crowd or to speak before others. The great Bodhisattva Chenrezig was so moved by compassion that he blessed his name to enable others to overcome fear simply by repeating it three times.

We might think it is too difficult to be so concerned for others but this is not sufficient reason for giving up. Radical changes in our attitudes are possible, as we can see from the fact that someone whose name once caused us fear and horror can become such a close friend that we cannot bear to live without them. Our attitudes are a question of habit, and it is definitely possible to become familiar with the wish to protect others.

Chapter 5

Transforming Attitudes

If we continue to cherish only ourselves, we will always be afraid. Our self-concern makes us worry about what might happen, even when nothing is threatening us. We are terrified by snakes and scorpions, which are, in fact, quite minor causes of fear. To alleviate our hunger and thirst we cause the death of many creatures. Greed in our search for prosperity and happiness makes us ruin forests, rivers and mountains, and even when we are not doing it ourselves, our many needs and desires insure that others will continue to exploit these natural resources without thinking about the long-term consequences. When we destroy the habitat of non-humans, such as certain kinds of celestial beings and nagas,[1] they respond by harming us, causing disease, conflict in the home and other troubles. Clearly a radical change in our attitude is needed.

Attachment to our body and self makes us cling to our wealth and think, "If I give this away, what will be left for me?" Such an attitude is responsible for all our problems, while the thought, "If I use this, I'll have nothing to give to others," is responsible for all joy and well-being. If we strive for fame, praise and respect, we will be reborn as some inferior creature or a person whom others despise. If we insure that others receive praise, fame, service and regard, it will lead to a good rebirth in which we enjoy status, a good appearance and others' respect. If we exploit others for our own benefit, we will be exploited and manipulated in another life, but if we use our physical and mental resources to care for others, we will also be taken care of, not only in future but also in this life.

Without reversing our present attitudes towards ourselves and others, we cannot attain enlightenment. We might think, "Well, so what?" But at the same time we don't want to remain in our present condition, experiencing unhappiness and suffering. By considering all these points carefully, we will realize that making this switch in our attitudes is possible. This is what "exchanging self and others" means.

It doesn't mean regarding the other person as oneself or feeling that one actually is the other, or that their body is actually one's own. Previously we have neglected others and cherished ourselves at their expense. Now we should resolve to cherish others and neglect our own selfish interests. Having thought deeply about the faults of selfishness and the benefits of cherishing others, we will understand the former as the root of all our misfortunes and the latter as the source of all well-being. This understanding will fuel our wish to make the switch in attitude.

Till now all our efforts have been concentrated on accomplishing our own happiness. Now we will concentrate entirely on making others happy. We have always ignored them but from now on we will forget about ourselves. We need strength not to be discouraged by the thought of taking on every form of suffering experienced by living beings. Unable to tolerate even their most minor suffering, we will be prepared to alleviate it, no matter how much time and difficulty are involved. All our energy will be directed towards this. Such an attitude results from understanding just how limiting and harmful selfishness is and how truly cherishing others brings joy and many hitherto unimagined benefits.

In his *Great Exposition of the Stages of the Path* Je Tsongkhapa first defines what is meant by "equalizing" and then explains how to cultivate this state of mind. He encourages us to persevere with thinking about the disadvantages of not cherishing others and the great advantages of doing so, as a way to develop greater enthusiasm. He defines what exchange of self and others means, describes the main obstacles that prevent us from making this switch and how to overcome them. As a result of deeply contemplating the faults of self-concern and the benefits of cherishing others, this reversal will come about automatically.

However hopeless the condition of living beings may appear, they all have the capacity to become free from suffering and to enjoy happiness because of their inner potential and the purity of their nature. Though we may really wish to remove their suffering and give them happiness, what we are able to do at present is extremely limited. From this we see how important our own enlightenment is. Our hope to become enlightened will only make us act if we are convinced that it is really possible to overcome our faults and limitations and to develop our full potential. We must understand what enlightenment entails, realize that we have the ability to attain it and then resolve to do so. Others' well-being is our primary reason for doing this, but enlightenment is also the full flowering of our own potential. As long as we think it is sufficient merely to stop our personal suffering, we will not aspire to gain the wisdom body of an enlightened being.

What are the obstacles to exchanging self and others? At present we see our own self, the basis for our personal happiness and suffering, and the self of others, the basis of their happiness and suffering, as quite unrelated, rather like blue and yellow, which can be taken to mind without reference to each other. Because of this we are not concerned about their happiness and suffering, while our own condition is of immense importance to us. Though we and they are of course different, we are nevertheless connected. It is impossible to conceive of "self" except in relation to "other," just as "this side" only makes sense in relation to "that side" and vice versa. They are mutually dependent. "This side" is only this side while we are here, but when we get over there, our perspective has changed. Neither self nor other are inherently existent. What am I, self or other? Both thoughts are valid in relation to me.

We may think others' suffering doesn't hurt us so why should we bother to alleviate it. If this is the argument we use, there are two analogies which can help us to change our attitude. Why should we do anything to alleviate the suffering we will experience when we are old, such as saving money or buying insurance policies, because that suffering doesn't affect us now? Why should our hand do anything to help when we have a thorn in the foot? After all the thorn isn't hurting our hand. We shouldn't be too quick to dismiss these examples. Exploring them in meditation can help to bring about a change in our way of thinking.

We may argue that in the first case the young person and the old person are part of the same continuum, while in the second the hand and foot are both body parts belonging to the same collection and are therefore intimately related. A continuum is a collection of former and later moments and a collection is an aggregation of parts. For example, a rosary and an army are attributions made respectively to a collection of beads and a group of men. When we search for the rosary or the army, we can't find them. This shows they are false in that they appear to exist from their own side but do not. If things existed in and of themselves as they appear to do, they should be findable. The fact that they aren't demonstrates that they do not exist as they appear. Self and other are also mere attributions without any existence from their own side. No matter what we look at, it seems to exist objectively and we assent to this appearance.

The "I" doesn't seem to be a mere attribution to body and mind but existent in and of itself. In fact our own self and the other person's self are mere attributions to a continuum of earlier and later moments and are not discrete inherently existent entities. Contemplation of these ideas can be helpful in breaking down our exaggerated self-concern, which stems from a misconception of the self. This misconception produces our compulsive quest for happiness through satisfaction of the senses, through possessions, friends, status and so forth. When we fail to secure the happiness we seek, we experience frustration, anger and suffering.

Will understanding the true nature of the self stop our longing for worldly happiness and bring about a transformation in our attitudes? There are many levels to understanding the true nature of the self. Even a recognition that the self undergoes change moment by moment will dramatically decrease our preoccupation with the things of this life. Because of our clinging to the self as enduring and unchanging, we waste our energy on trivial concerns and neglect what is important.

We accept appearances whereby things seem independent of causes and conditions and parts. When we gain the insight that everything exists dependently and become accustomed to perceiving things in that way, our conception of true objective existence will be weakened to such an extent that it can no longer give rise to attachment and aversion. We will see the possibility of getting rid of this misconception altogether and will also recognize that others suffer like us through their misconception of the self. Understanding the true nature of the self loosens the root of our suffering. It brings about a profound transformation in outlook. As long as the root of our suffering remains firmly embedded and intact, all our attempts to find happiness will fail.

If we don't correctly identify what is poisoning our life and instead nurture it, happiness will continue to elude us. We have it the wrong way round. If someone asks why we are unhappy, we have a long list of people and circumstances to blame. Very few of us will point to something within. The law recognizes the harmful effects of the disturbing emotions only in their crudest aspects when they lead to blatant dishonesty, rape, robbery, violence and murder. Nobody but a true spiritual practitioner will mention the need to uproot those disturbing emotions in all their forms and yet, if we are honest, we must admit how upsetting they are and how much misery they cause us. No matter how luxurious our surroundings, these emotions will prevent us from enjoying comfort and from getting a good night's sleep. And even if we do sleep, we wake up miserable in the morning. How much happier we and those around us would be if we could stop the grosser manifestations of these emotions.

Our self-concern makes us consider even minor discomforts unbearable. Reversing this, our aim is to become as sensitive to others' slightest suffering as we are to our own. To prepare the ground for this, we contemplate the faults of selfishness and the benefits of cherishing others, so that we can develop a real wish for change and identify the obstacles which stand in its way.

Until now we have suffered long and intensely in cyclic existence because of our attachment to the self. Our egotism leads to negative physical, verbal and mental habits with all sorts of unwanted consequences for others. It makes us ignore the distinction between virtue and non-virtue and thereby kills our chances of a good rebirth and liberation. It strips us of everything and leaves us naked and empty-handed.

A healthy interest in our own welfare is fine, but far from accomplishing our well-being, our exclusive concern with it has simply produced endless suffering. We can observe how hard humans and animals try to find happiness and yet they all experience suffering. We fail to find happiness because we use the wrong methods. Our selfishness cuts us off from present and future happiness but we don't recognize this as the real obstacle. We don't blame our misconceptions and egoism but instead blame others.

We magnify the importance of the self and our own happiness and have unrealistic expectations. Our reputation means a lot to us. We may want to be known as a good meditator, a fine scholar, a monk or nun who observes ethical discipline really well or as someone who is always kind, generous and helpful to others. To accomplish this we are often prepared to act negatively and emotions like pride, envy, disdain and competitiveness arise easily. We cannot bear to see others doing well in any way and a single word or look can make us burn with rage.

We are most reluctant to admit our faults, but until we can face our own imperfections, our study and practice of the teachings will not bear fruit because egoism is in conflict with the teachings and with decent human conduct. We easily observe such behavior in others but think we are fine just the way we are. Unless we recognize the same pattern in ourselves, we will not benefit from the teachings nor from the presence and care of our teachers. When friends offer us useful advice and point out our faults, we see their criticism as interference and refuse to accept advice. Our response antagonizes others and we soon find ourselves at odds with those around us. Before very long it seems as if the whole world is hostile. We feel more and more isolated and friendless. All this happens because we do not value others and think only of ourselves.

We all know the kind of people who are so preoccupied with themselves that they talk of nothing else. They don't purposely ignore one, but their minds are totally taken up with their own experiences and activities. Between countries, between members of a community, within the family, between teachers and students, mutual respect and consideration are of greatest importance.

If we had invested as much energy in alleviating others' suffering and giving them happiness as we have in the pursuit of personal happiness, we would have accomplished our own and others' well-being long ago. There isn't a shred of doubt about this. Instead all our effort has been wasted and futile.

Now resolve not to continue like this. Think, "May I be clear now and in future about the true identity of my enemy. May I always bear it in mind. May I prevent all future selfish thoughts and actions and may I stop all my present selfishness now." Only by expelling our misconception of the self and our selfishness can we truly fulfill our human potential. We should take pride in combating our selfishness. Once we get rid of it, it will automatically be replaced by concern for others.

There are two parts to our minds: the part responsible for all our troubles and disasters and the part which brings all happiness. To transform we must distinguish clearly between them. Acting to prevent self-concern from arising, stopping any manifestations of it as quickly as possible, cultivating new forms of concern for others and strengthening our present expressions of it will bring about the change we desire. If we are bored by this list of the faults of selfishness, it is because we have no real desire to change our ways, but instead want to hear something new and exotic.

The crux of these instructions is constantly to try not to be influenced by attachment to "our own side." We are training ourselves to give everything—our property, body and positive energy without any hope of reward or return. If we hope for anything in return, even a good rebirth or enlightenment, it is just like a business transaction. Making a small outlay we hope for large returns. If we could learn to be as generous as Bodhisattvas, we would find that all our needs are met.

As beginners we must practice in imagination sincerely giving everything to others and dedicating our physical, verbal and mental actions to their service. In practice we shouldn't overreach ourselves but do what is within our capacity. Nor need we feel compelled to do everything others ask of us. It is important to protect ourselves, for if we are weakened, we can help nobody. At present we are as fragile as a bubble and don't have much stamina.

Having promised everything to others, we must serve them faithfully and must not wrong them by looking at or speaking to them in a hurtful way, nor by thinking harmful thoughts. Any self-serving impulses we notice, we should try to stop at once, for these are the cause of all our troubles.

Who can criticize this practice? We may feel it is too difficult for us, but if we make an effort to begin, gradually we will be able to do more and more. Admiration for such conduct, feeling inspired by it and making prayers that one day we will be able to act like this ourselves is the first step. Do we learn about such things in school? Most of us think we are quite clever and capable. This is a good way to use our intelligence and aptitudes.

It's important not just to cling to one small practice. We can't expect to accomplish a vast result when the cause we create is limited. Moreover, if by chance we are not doing that practice correctly, we will end up with nothing. It is essential to see the whole picture and implant predispositions for the complete path. Since this may seem overwhelming, we need the good sense to find our own level. We should practice step by step, concentrating on what is appropriate at our particular stage of development, but always briefly reviewing the complete path as well.

Appreciating the progress we make will give us encouragement. If we used to kill mosquitoes without a second thought but now try to catch and remove them, that is a positive step forward. How easy it is to take revenge on a mosquito! How good to refrain! All our temporary and ultimate wishes will be fulfilled by changing our attitude and this is how it begins. There is no better way to please those who are intent on others' well-being. If we hurt the living beings they are trying to help, how can our gifts please them? If we reject all this from the outset, we aren't giving ourselves a fair chance.

As has already been mentioned, in the seven-step cause and effect sequence we think about the past kindness of living beings when they have been our mothers, whereas here we remember their kindness at all times and our total dependence on them. We also reflect on the fact that they are the source of all our temporary and ultimate happiness. These are good reasons for cherishing them. Even if we disregard the attainment of a high rebirth, liberation and enlightenment, it is easy to see that we depend on other living beings for the food we eat, the clothes we wear and our shelter. For our bowl of rice many living beings have given their lives or been injured and others have labored. The wool for the "pure new wool" clothes we like to wear came from the back of a sheep and many people worked to make it into a garment. In many countries animals as well as people toil when a house is built.

A good rebirth depends on ethical discipline, which can only be practiced in relation to others. All the circumstances which would make such a rebirth comfortable depend on generosity, patience and other virtues which cannot develop without others. Since others are our wish-fulfilling jewels, we should cherish and nurture them as we would look after a fertile field, knowing that whatever seed we sow in it will yield a bountiful crop. Shantideva says:

> Thus the state of buddhahood depends
> On beings and the buddhas equally.
> By what tradition is it then
> That buddhas, but not beings, are revered?

By seeing the enormous drawbacks of self-centeredness, we will develop the ability to see all beings as lovable. The Kadampa master Geshe Bengungyel[2] was constantly on the look-out for signs of his selfishness. Once during a monastic ceremony very thick rich curd was offered to the participants. Bengungyel was sitting in the middle of the gathering and when he saw big ladlefuls being doled out, he began to worry that there would be none left by the time his turn came. As soon as he noticed this selfish thought, he turned his bowl upside down and pulled his top robe over his head. When they wanted to serve him and asked whether he wasn't having any, he refused saying, "My bad mind has already eaten the curd!"

On another occasion when his benefactor was coming to visit, he spent more time than usual carefully arranging the offerings on his shrine. When he realized his motivation wasn't pure, he picked up a handful of ash and threw it over the offerings. The Indian master Padampa Sangye,[3] who had clairvoyant powers, remarked, "Today the best offerings in the whole of Tibet were made by Geshe Bengungyel, who has thrown ash in the mouth of the eight worldly concerns."[4]

In his writing another Kadampa master, Geshe Potowa,[5] says that he had only ever thought of others' profit and happiness and had never wished for these just for himself. As a child he used to go to a crossroads and with each person that passed he would make the prayer, "May the places this person is coming from and going to enjoy prosperity and peace and may his wishes be fulfilled." When he was very small he was upset to see the wind blowing the dead leaves along because he thought they were little animals, until an adult explained.

As soon as concern for others becomes constant and spontaneous we have made the switch. The practice of giving and taking is used to strengthen our love and compassion. With sufficient familiarity this can be done as we breathe. As we inhale, we breathe in the suffering of others and as we exhale, we send them our happiness and well-being. If we keep doing this practice with sincerity, our love and compassion for others will certainly grow.

When we intend to do a session of giving and taking, the six preliminaries[6] should first be performed. We clean and tidy our surroundings and the room where we will meditate, set up representations of enlightened body, speech and mind, arrange offerings of water, flowers, incense, light, perfume and food as beautifully as possible and, sitting on a comfortable seat in a good meditation position, we take refuge and arouse the altruistic intention. Adopting a good meditation position is valuable, but even more important is to make sure our mind is in a positive state and that our altruistic motivation is intense enough to warm the whole practice.

We then imagine "the field of accumulation,"[7] all those in whom we take refuge and in relation to whom we create merit. Next we perform the seven-part practice[8] and offer the mandala.[9] The seven-part practice is a powerful way of accumulating positive energy through paying homage and making offerings, through rejoicing, requesting the teachings, beseeching our teachers not to leave the world and through dedication. Purification takes the form of acknowledging wrong-doing. This is what Bodhisattvas did in the past when they came from other places to see the Buddha, and Tibetans today still behave in a similar manner when they have the opportunity to meet His Holiness the Dalai Lama.

We should not regard this seven-part practice as unimportant. For example, if we understand how to make prostrations properly and the advantages of doing so, we will realize what a vast practice it can be. We make prostrations and offerings for our own benefit and not for the benefit of those to whom we show respect, for, even if we think only of this life, creating positive energy removes obstacles and allows us to accomplish our wishes. There are ways of showing homage and respect in every culture and we should not feel that doing so demeans us in any way.

The requests we make are for the enlightened ones and Bodhisattvas to bless us so that we may develop qualities of knowledge, compassion and power which are like theirs. We imagine that they are pleased with this request and radiate light and nectar which enters through the crown of our head, purifying all negativities and obstacles and increasing our life-force, merit and good qualities.

They remain in the space before us and, filled with a sense of their blessings, we imagine around us all living beings in human form but experiencing the suffering of their respective realms of existence. It is easier to imagine them as human beings. When we think of them suffering, it arouses our compassion. We remember our close connection to them, and seeing them as near, dear and lovable, we contemplate their suffering until a strong wish to free them from it arises.

With this compassion we imagine taking on their suffering—and the contaminated actions and disturbing emotions which cause it—in the form of a black stream or laser beam which strikes and decimates the selfishness in our heart. We take the suffering from them as if we were shaving it off. It leaves them through the right nostril and enters us through the left, striking the selfishness, which can be visualized as a black lump, a heap of charred paper or a flame that is extinguished by the black stream. We use whichever image we find most powerful.

If we have a particular problem or a sickness, we may think there are many others in the world who are afflicted in the same way. Making a strong wish that our own suffering might replace theirs, we take it from them in a black stream which strikes the site of our own sickness and destroys it. When there is something we can do about our suffering, we should turn our energy to making changes, but when there is nothing we can do, this practice can help us mentally and sometimes also relieves physical pain. At least it gives us a way of using the pain positively.

While someone is suffering, they cannot experience pleasure. We therefore remove suffering first and then give happiness. The taking practice can be done on its own and need not necessarily be followed by giving. Of the two, taking the suffering is the more important practice.

Imagining we have freed others from suffering and feeling satisfied with what we have done, we now think about their lack of happiness until a strong wish to see them happy arises. With this love we give them our well-being and the virtue which causes it in the form of a white light that leaves through our right nostril and enters them through their left nostril. We imagine that we have bestowed temporary and ultimate well-being on them and we feel joy at having done this.

Although our aim is to see all living beings as lovable, it is undeniable that at present we do not see them in this way. For this reason we should begin the giving and taking practice with someone who is near and dear, whose difficulties we do actually want to alleviate and to whom we want to give happiness. If we focus on such a person our practice is more likely to be wholehearted.

In fact, however, Geshe Chekawa's *Seven Points for Training the Mind* tells us to begin with ourselves. If we are doing the practice in the morning, we imagine taking on our own suffering of the evening in a black stream which strikes and destroys the selfishness in our heart. We then give the morning's well-being in the form of white light to the person we will be in the evening. We take on next week's suffering this week, next year's suffering this year and the suffering of future lives in this one. Having practiced on ourselves, we next focus on family and friends, then on neutral people and finally on those we dislike and consider hostile. In each case we should try to do what we can to help in practical ways as well.

Many of the great texts recommend that we start with our mother of this life. This is helpful if we have enjoyed a close and loving relationship with her; otherwise we should choose someone with whom we have had such a relationship, and arouse compassion and love in a very personal and intense way.

Where harmful humans, spirits or animals are concerned, we should imagine them clearly before us. It is difficult to feel closeness and affection for them. Yet they were our mothers many times in the past, doing everything in their power to protect us from pain and give us happiness. While doing this they endured many hardships and performed many negative actions. They had no opportunity to develop spiritually, which is why they are harmful now.

Since they do not remember this close relationship with us and are unaware that we have been kind and nurtured them, they harm us, which insures that they will suffer in the future. In a way we are a cause of their suffering because in the past they were involved in looking after us. Now we are a target for their harm because of our own past actions. Responsible as we therefore are for their condition, we should feel compassion towards them and strongly wish that they might be free from suffering and enjoy happiness in the future.

We can see only humans and animals but there are many spirits. If we feel spirits are causing harm, we should invite them to come before us and say the following: "In past lives I have eaten your flesh, drunk your blood and worn your skin. Now I will repay my debt." If we feel afraid of this practice, we imagine expelling our consciousness via the crown of our heads in the form of a white syllable *HRI* or white light. Our body grows bigger, fatter and more juicy. We cut it open and lay it out before them. We offer it, saying, "If you want meat, eat my flesh. If you want to drink, drink my blood. Here are my bones to gnaw on and my skin to wear. If you're in a hurry eat me raw but if you have time, cook me and use me in whatever way you want."

If we are really courageous, we do this practice without first expelling our consciousness. We imagine that, having feasted, their malevolence subsides and they are full of love because they feel completely satisfied and content. When this has been accomplished, we visualize that our body is not only restored but finer and healthier than before. If we expelled our consciousness, we imagine it re-entering our body. When

this practice is done with sincerity, harm really does subside. At present we do it in our imagination and the great masters warn us that we must, in fact, protect our body until we are able to give it as easily as a vegetable!

We have so many different fears, all of which are rooted in self-concern. If we can let go of that, our fears will diminish. To overcome this self-concern and our misconception of the self we need to develop the conventional and ultimate altruistic intention. This is the best way of overcoming all fears, for if we appeal to some external force, we may find ourselves even more frightened and in a greater tangle.

When taking on suffering, we can imagine the specific suffering of each realm. When training ourselves to give, we imagine giving our body, possessions and positive energy. Our body becomes a wish-fulfilling jewel, transforming into whatever is needed by living creatures and by the environment. To those in the hot hells we give our body in the form of rain, which extinguishes the fires and brings them coolness. We also imagine giving them our body in the form of a precious human rebirth with which to practice, in the form of celestial mansions in which to live, as food and clothing and as spiritual teachers to instruct them, so that they can attain liberation and enlightenment. This is how we imagine fulfilling all their temporary and ultimate needs.

We give in this way to all beings throughout all the realms of existence. When taking on suffering, we should not imagine doing so from Buddhas and our spiritual teachers but when giving we can include everyone. When giving to the Buddhas, Bodhisattvas and to our teachers we imagine our body turning into clouds of offerings. Once we have gained facility with giving and taking, it should be done as we breathe in and out. This will help us to develop the altruistic intention more quickly.

Sometimes we can practice focusing on living beings in a particular area or country, or on those who live uphill or downhill from us. We hear so much bad news about suffering in different parts of the world and, although in many cases there is nothing practical we can do, this practice can make us feel a little less helpless.

If you were seriously ill and someone came to help you, wouldn't it be comforting to know they were prepared to do anything they could to alleviate your suffering and give you happiness? It would help to make you feel better, even if there wasn't much they could do physically. Think of two nurses: one is very efficient and good at her work. She fulfills her duties and earns her living honestly. The other nurse does exactly the same work with love and compassion. Don't you think you would feel the difference? Her work has become a spiritual practice.

Geshe Chekawa's text tells us to train ourselves in the practice of giving and taking by means of the words. We can take inspiration from Nagarjuna's *Precious Garland*,[10] but we can also make up our own words. What we aren't capable of doing now, we should pray to do in future, and repeat the words of giving and taking again and again.

Through doing this sincerely the resolve to take personal responsibility for others' well-being eventually arises. With that special wish in our hearts, we repeat our commitment to living beings in words. From our refuge practice we will understand the qualities which make it possible for enlightened beings to accomplish others' welfare. Appreciation of their qualities will inspire us to develop the altruistic intention to attain enlightenment for others' sake.

This concludes the instructions on how to develop the altruistic intention. There are eleven steps: equanimity, recognizing all beings as our mothers, remembering their kindness, repaying their kindness, equalizing self and others, recognizing selfishness as the enemy, seeing the benefits of cherishing others, giving to strengthen love and taking to strengthen compassion, both of which are combined with the thought of exchanging self and others, the special wish and the altruistic intention.[11]

Chapter 6

How to Hold the
Altruistic Intention

When as a result of our intense love and compassion the wish to attain enlightenment for the sake of all living beings is present in everything we do, our physical and verbal actions will create inexhaustible merit. At that point we have developed the aspiring altruistic intention and can take part in a ceremony through which we formally affirm our aspiration to attain complete enlightenment. Simply doing this creates tremendous positive energy.

It is also possible to participate in this ceremony with a deeper level of involvement, making a commitment never to give up the altruistic intention until we attain enlightenment and to observe the precepts associated with the aspiring altruistic intention to prevent its decline. The spiritual teacher who confers these precepts should hold them and should also hold the Bodhisattva vow. The ritual is not hard to perform, but those who are properly qualified in this respect are rare. For this reason people are normally eager to receive the precepts from His Holiness the Dalai Lama, who fulfills these important criteria.

Ideally the recipient should already have developed the altruistic intention and wish to affirm it through the ceremony.

However, since this too is rare, we should at least have some experience in the practices of the initial level, such as recognizing the preciousness of our human life of freedom and fortune, understanding its transient nature, taking heartfelt refuge in the Three Jewels and gaining conviction regarding the connection between actions and their effects. We also need to have a sound knowledge of the practices of the intermediate level, such as contemplating the dissatisfactory nature of any state within cyclic existence, understanding the process by which we keep taking involuntary rebirth and what constitutes the training in ethical discipline, concentration and wisdom through which we can free ourselves from cyclic existence. This should lead to a keen sense of our own transience as well as a strong wish to get out of cyclic existence.

When the spiritual teacher tries to arouse the altruistic intention in us during the ceremony, we should be able to respond with feeling. His Holiness the Dalai Lama does this very skillfully and again and again urges us to allow a sincere wish to attain enlightenment for the sake of living beings to arise. We should be more than mere spectators, otherwise how can we speak of holding the altruistic intention and the precepts?

The ceremony has three parts: the preparation, the actual ritual and the conclusion. The preparation consists of taking refuge in a special way, creating positive energy and preparing our mind by arousing love and compassion.

Taking refuge in a special way entails first of all making ready the place where the ceremony is to be held. A peaceful and pleasing place where there are no disturbances nor people hostile to the Buddha's teachings should be chosen for the ceremony. After cleaning and making it fragrant with sandalwood and incense and adorning it with flowers and other decorations, representations of enlightened body, speech and mind are set up. A consecrated statue or painting of the Buddha represents enlightened body, a *stupa*[1] represents enlightened mind and a volume of Mahayana scriptures, preferably one of the Perfection of Wisdom sutras such as the *Heart Sutra*, represents enlightened speech. A canopy is hung over these representations and in front of them lavish, beautiful and honestly acquired offerings, fine enough to astonish one's friends, are carefully arranged. Members of the spiritual community are invited to read the Perfection of Wisdom sutras to create merit. They are offered food and shown respect.

When Atisha was asked to give the precepts in Samye,[2] he remarked that the offerings were unsatisfactory. Undoubtedly they were lavish, as was the custom in Tibet, but perhaps they were made with a tainted motivation. Often there was so much food that it could not all be distributed and unfortunately had to be thrown away. When His Holiness the Dalai Lama was teaching the *Essence of Refined Gold*,[3] a text on the graduated stages of the path, at Norbulingka[4] in Tibet, he gave the Bodhisattva vow, after which an offering ceremony was held. There was so much food to give away that everyone present received a huge amount and in the end cartloads were sent to the monastic universities of Sera, Drepung and Ganden.[5]

Those who intend to participate in the ceremony wash, put on clean clothes and conduct themselves with dignity befitting the occasion. When we are taking part in an important secular event, we dress up and at New Year Tibetan people often wear new clothes. Since this is an important spiritual occasion, we should honor it in a similar way. Ordained people do so by wearing both yellow robes and lay people wear their best clothes.

The spiritual teacher invites the assembly of exalted ones, the Buddhas and Bodhisattvas, blesses the offerings and describes the inspiring qualities of the assembly of exalted beings. Visualizing them, the participants perform the seven-part practice. Some masters say that not all seven parts should be performed, since on this occasion it would be depressing to recall our negative actions and that only prostrations and offerings should be made because it is important to feel joyful. Seeing the spiritual teacher in the form of the Buddha, we offer the mandala. Kneeling with our right knee touching the ground and with our hands placed together in the gesture of supplication, we request refuge. The teacher then says the words by which one takes refuge and we repeat them. We take refuge in the enlightened ones, in their teachings and in the spiritual community of Bodhisattvas who will never give up the enlightened intention.[6] Seeing the jewel of the enlightened ones as those who show us the true refuge, the jewel of the teachings as our actual refuge[7] and the jewel of the spiritual community as our role-models and support, we take refuge until we attain the heart or essence of enlightenment, which means the wisdom truth body of an enlightened being, for the sole purpose of protecting living beings.

Once we have taken refuge formally in this way, the spiritual teacher then instructs us in the precepts to be followed. These consist of certain things that should and should not be done in relation to each of the Three Jewels individually and in relation to all three in general.[8]

The next preparation is the creation of positive energy, which is done by once more performing the seven-part practice. Words from the *King of Prayers*[9] or from Shantideva's *Way of the Bodhisattva* may be used. The final preparation is to make our mind ready by arousing affection for all living beings. Without this our compassion will be partial. In his *Lamp for the Path to Enlightenment* Atisha stresses the importance of arousing the kind of love for living beings which sees them as near and dear. Having done this we contemplate the suffering of those in the three bad states of rebirth. Atisha says:

> Next, beginning with an attitude
> Of love for all living creatures,
> Consider beings, excluding none,
> Suffering in the three bad rebirths—
> Suffering birth, death and so forth.

> Then, since you want to free these beings
> From the suffering of pain,
> From suffering and the causes of suffering,
> Arouse immutably the resolve
> To attain enlightenment.

Those in the hells suffer from intense heat and cold. Hungry spirits are famished, parched and fearful. Animals suffer from stupidity and ignorance. They also experience terror because of larger predators and because smaller animals band together and eat bigger ones.

We think about our human suffering of birth, ageing, sickness and death, and of how we don't get what we want but instead experience much that is unwanted. We reflect on the suffering of celestial beings of the desire realm who enjoy sensual pleasures till the signs of death begin to appear. Their radiance fades, their clothes become wrinkled and old, they start to stink, their garlands wilt and their friends no longer want to come near them. Since they have clairvoyant powers they know from which rebirth they have come and to which they are going. Although they experience no physical suffering, when they foresee their rebirth as a human or in one of the unhappy states, they feel anguish. We also think of the suffering of celestial beings of the form and formless realms who have no control over how long they can remain in those states. Living beings in cyclic existence experience the suffering of pain, the suffering of change and the pervasive suffering of conditioning.

A strong feeling of compassion that wants to free them from all forms of suffering arises. This is followed by the altruistic intention which focuses first and foremost on the welfare of others and on our own enlightenment only as a means to accomplish it. Rescuing others from danger or suffering and insuring their safety and comfort clearly helps them in this life. If we show them how to attain a good rebirth, we have looked after them for more than one life. Here we are concerned with their ultimate happiness and freedom from all suffering. If we cannot bear to see others suffer or get involved in doing what will cause them suffering, we would obviously never hurt them intentionally. Such compassion would change the places where we live and the lives of others—both people and animals—who come into contact with us.

In his most concise exposition of the stages of the path[10] Je Tsongkhapa says: "The altruistic intention is the mainstay of the supreme vehicle, the foundation and basis of its powerful activities. Like an elixir that turns the two stores to gold, it's a treasure of merit comprising every kind of good. Knowing this, heroic Bodhisattvas make this precious and supreme attitude their quintessential practice. This is what I, the practitioner, have done, and you, who seek liberation, should do likewise."

The altruistic intention is the main road to enlightenment which all Buddhas of the past have taken and all Buddhas to come will take. It is the basis for all Bodhisattva activities, such as practice of the six perfections, which cause us to become truly mature, and practice of the four ways of ripening others, through which we help them to become mature.[11]

All these activities create the two great stores of positive energy and insight. The two kinds of form bodies which enlightened beings manifest for the benefit of others result from the great store of positive energy of which the chief source is the conventional altruistic intention. The wisdom body, which represents the fulfillment of an enlightened being's own fullest potential, results from the store of insights of which the most important is the understanding of reality. However, this insight only acts as a cause for enlightenment if it is supported by the altruistic intention. The altruistic intention is like a vast reservoir of inexhaustible virtue. This is why Bodhisattvas make it their essential practice.

PREVENTING THE ALTRUISTIC INTENTION FROM DECLINING

During the ceremony of affirming our altruistic intention and taking the precepts, we see our spiritual teacher as the

Buddha and call upon him or her and all enlightened beings and Bodhisattvas before us to act as witnesses. After the words of the ceremony have been repeated, the spiritual teacher explains the precepts which we have undertaken to observe. Four of these are intended to help prevent the altruistic intention from declining in this life.

The first is to maintain enthusiasm for the altruistic intention by thinking of its great benefits again and again. Since most of us don't yet have the altruistic intention, we should think of the benefits of kindness and the disadvantages of being unkind.

The second precept is to increase the strength of our altruistic intention by training ourselves in it three times a day and three times a night.

The third precept is to train ourselves never to abandon a single being. Our promise is to attain enlightenment for all living beings, therefore no matter how they behave or what they do to us, we should never abandon them.

The fourth is to make effort to create the two great stores of positive energy and insight.

These four precepts, which are drawn from the great texts that deal with Bodhisattva conduct, present us with much food for thought and meditation practice. When such great texts are taught we often feel overwhelmed by a wealth of detail and there is a distinct danger that we may see them as suitable for intellectual study but not as a source for practice. We may then go in search of something short, easy and uncomplicated to use for meditation, which is a big mistake. We must learn how to study the great texts and draw from them what we need for meditation.

Maintaining Enthusiasm

In order to keep the first of these precepts we must recognize the benefits which the altruistic intention brings. These have already been discussed but it is useful to remind ourselves of them again and again. The altruistic intention is the door to the Great Vehicle and the basis for all profound and extensive Bodhisattva deeds. Any action supported by the altruistic intention acts as a cause for enlightenment. Celestial beings and humans revere, cherish and lavish gifts on those who have the altruistic intention. It protects from internal and external obstacles. White forces and protectors will look after those who possess it, since they embody the heart of the teachings in their lives and through this bring benefit to the world. Malevolent beings will either not think of harming such a person or if they do, they will not succeed in doing damage.

Buddhas regard those with the altruistic intention as their children and Bodhisattvas regard them as their siblings. They pray that this sublime intention may be fulfilled. Their greatest hope is that we may become kinder. When we do, it is an offering of accomplishment far finer and more pleasing than any material offering.

Sickness and obstacles, which others find hard to pacify with rituals and mantras, will quickly be removed through the altruistic intention, and the four kinds of activity—peaceful, increasing, powerful and fierce—will easily be accomplished. In the place where someone who possesses the altruistic intention lives, there will be less sickness, famine and fear, and should they occur, they will not last long. That place will be venerated, not because the stones or earth are inherently more sacred than in other places but because it has been sanctified by the practitioner. For this to happen the practitioner must be a holy person, a true practitioner. Such a place becomes sacred and has the power to bless those who visit it on pilgrimage by acting as an inspiration for their own spiritual practice.

The body and mind of those with the altruistic intention is fully serviceable, which prevents physical and mental exhaustion when they exert themselves for others. They will definitely be patient and tolerant and will not take revenge when harmed by others. In fact, when they see the one who has perpetrated harm under attack, they will intervene to protect him. They will rarely experience anger, jealousy, pride or the wish to hide their faults. When they do, these emotions will be short-lived.

They will not suffer physical or mental harm after death and are unlikely to take a bad rebirth. Even if they do, they will suffer less and out of compassion help those around them. It is said they will quickly bounce out of the bad rebirth like a ball. Cultivating mindfulness and mental alertness is essential if we want to develop our good qualities and get rid of faults. While distraction and the disturbing emotions rule our minds, the physical and verbal actions we perform lack the power to be of great benefit to others. The wound of our mind is much more vulnerable than any physical wound. We must watch over it as carefully as we would take care of a physical wound while in the company of rough people. Purity and impurity, the environment and living beings are all products of our mind. Since transformation can only take place if we desire it, thinking about the benefits of kindheartedness can inspire us to become kinder. Physical and verbal actions based on kindness create powerful benefit.

The possibility of improvement is apparent when we consider our own mind. Sometimes we are in a black mood and full of turbulent emotions, but our mind isn't black through and through like coal. At other times we feel peaceful. It is not hard to recognize which is the better and more constructive state of mind. When we are peaceful our actions are calm, which brings us and those around us happiness.

If the altruistic intention had physical form, space could not contain it. This is because it focuses on all living beings without excepting a single one. With it we wish to free them, not from particular kinds of suffering, but from every form of suffering they experience and to provide them with every kind of temporary and ultimate happiness. Could anything be more positive? If we look after a friend who is sick, provide him with medicine and nurse him back to health, we have done something very good. In the case of the altruistic intention, since the aspiration is vast, the virtue it creates is also vast. Our human mind has immense potential for good and evil. Seated where we are, we can create intense virtue or non-virtue in a single moment.

Strengthening the Intention

The second precept that we promise to observe, when we formally affirm our aspiration, reminds us that once we have aroused enthusiasm for the altruistic intention by considering its benefits, we should prevent it from declining and strengthen it by recalling our intention three times during the day and three times during the night.

We might have second thoughts when we reflect on the countless number of living beings, on their behavior, on how we will have to work for them for an immensely long time and on how difficult it is to create the essential stores of insight and positive energy. How can we possibly take personal responsibility to free ALL living beings from suffering and give them happiness? We might feel discouraged and decide to work only for our own liberation. At that point we have given up the aspiring altruistic intention, which is more serious than transgressing any kind of individual liberation vow, such as the lay person's vow or the vow of a monk or nun. We have failed in our ethical discipline of working for others by putting our own interests first. With sound refuge and the altruistic intention, even if we indulge in sensual pleasures, the core of that ethical discipline remains intact.

If a blind beggar going through garbage comes across a jewel, a small miracle has happened for him and he will keep that jewel safe. We are like beggars and our body like a garbage heap of unclean substances in which we have discovered the priceless jewel-like altruistic intention. It can fulfill all our wishes, so we should cherish and hold on to it. We can cause it to grow by visualizing our spiritual teacher as the Buddha and calling on him, on all enlightened beings and all Bodhisattvas to act as witnesses while we reaffirm our commitment three times a day and three times a night. This may be done by repeating the words of the ceremony or by saying the verse of taking refuge and arousing the altruistic intention. Doing this at different intervals during the day and night helps us to remain constantly mindful of the altruistic intention and to develop intimate familiarity with it, so that the slightest circumstance will bring it to the fore. It is like stoking the fire by putting on more wood each time it burns low.

We have wasted many human lives in the past. Now, in this one, we must do the most important thing. Practicing the teachings is more important than just listening to them. Cherishing others is more important than cherishing oneself. Practicing in a secluded place is more important than being in the midst of busyness. Applying antidotes when the disturbing emotions arise is more important than avoiding the objects that stimulate them. As humans we have powerful bodies and minds and are capable of doing all of this.

The instructions for training the mind tell us to avoid various kinds of perverted activity. If someone were to take us to a secluded place and tell us to meditate on the teachings we have received, we would feel imprisoned, miserable and unwilling to bear the hardships involved, whereas we have endless patience for the hardships involved in putting down those we dislike, looking after friends, for business ventures and other worldly enterprises. This is perverted patience. Our aspirations are perverted since we aspire to wealth, rewards, reputation and respect instead of aspiring to free ourselves from cyclic existence. We long for the wrong experiences, wanting to savor ordinary pleasures instead of the effects of hearing, thinking about and meditating on the teachings, which would make our body and mind pliant and bring peace and happiness to us and others, both now and in the future. We may doubt this but it is absurd to dismiss the possibility if we have never tried it out.

Our compassion is perverted because we pity those who practice intensively and consider their way of life pathetic, while, in fact, our compassion should be directed towards those who suffer and constantly run after the causes of more suffering. We rejoice at the suffering that befalls the people we dislike but not at the causes for liberation which others create. We only need to look at ourselves to see whether all of this is true.

Not Abandoning Living Beings

The third precept, not to abandon living beings, means never giving up the hope of helping them even if they behave badly, hurt or disparage us. If we want to help others in general but exclude a particular individual, we have broken our promise. When others have caused us physical or mental suffering, we normally long for revenge. We wish them mishaps, suffering and unhappiness and we certainly have no wish ever to help them. Feeling like this undermines our altruistic intention and means we have abandoned those individuals. We may also feel that we can never again help a certain person who has been ungrateful for kindness we have shown him or her in the past. There may be no anger involved, only discouragement, but this too means that we have abandoned a living being.

Creating the Two Great Stores

The fourth precept is to support our altruistic intention through creating positive energy by making offerings to the Three Jewels and to our spiritual teachers. When we take refuge formally, one of the precepts is to make daily offerings of the first part of everything we eat and drink. We can also offer the beauty we see. If we find it difficult to offer this to enlightened beings because we cannot conceive of them, we can make the strong wish that all living beings should soon be able to enjoy such beauty. One of my spiritual teachers used to go on pilgrimage with his students and when they came to a particularly beautiful spot, they would all sit down some distance away, recite certain prayers and make an offering of it.

Building more muscle and developing our body is not of very great value—though, of course, it is good to keep healthy—but transforming our mind is definitely worthwhile. It means becoming more concerned about helping others, praising those who warrant it, learning to be generous, to protect others and to be patient. If we begin to do this while we are young, we will be happier, more tolerant and more relaxed when we are older.

MAINTAINING THE ALTRUISTIC INTENTION IN FUTURE LIVES

When Atisha was doing the longer circumambulation of the great stupa in Bodhgaya, thinking what practice would be most useful for the attainment of enlightenment, he saw two women ahead and overheard the younger ask the older what one must do to become enlightened. She answered, "Cultivate the altruistic intention." Later when he was in the temple within the stupa, he saw the small Buddha statues rise and ask the bigger ones what one must do to attain complete enlightenment. The answer was the same. In fact the two women were emanations of Tara[12] and the "Frowning One." These experiences persuaded Atisha of the immense importance of cultivating the altruistic intention. We may disbelieve these incidents but should remember that Atisha was not like us and not everything is as it seems to be. Good proof of this is that everything appears truly existent to us but isn't and all products seem stable yet they undergo change moment by moment.

Although these precepts are actually for Bodhisattvas who have developed the aspiring altruistic intention, we can begin to put them into practice now. Our first attempts at drawing, painting or at any craft may not be very impressive but with sufficient interest we can make rapid progress as we learn and practice. It's the same with the altruistic intention.

Having developed the altruistic intention, promised to maintain it and to prevent it from declining in this life by practicing these four precepts, we must also insure that we will not be separated from it in future lives. This is done by avoiding four kinds of black actions and cultivating four white ones.

Avoiding the Four Black Actions

The first black action is to tell lies to the person who has conferred the Bodhisattva vow on us, to our preceptors, spiritual teachers and to those who are worthy of offerings. Here the lie is, for instance, a conscious response to well-meant criticism. It is not important whether one succeeds in deceiving or not. Most people have a tendency to deviate from the truth when it is to their own advantage. Once we do that we are moving into the realm of falsehood. Some people are so devious that you never know what is going on. This kind of cleverness is in conflict with the Buddha's teachings and especially with those of the Great Vehicle because a Bodhisattva's conduct should be honest.

Why is it important not to lie to our spiritual teachers and why should we treat them in a special way? If we were blind and a surgeon operated on our eyes and gave us sight, we would be deeply grateful. Our spiritual teachers open our eye of wisdom. We enter into a relationship with them of our own free will and it is established by mutual consent. Through making offerings to them, we remember their kindness and show our gratitude. This is for our own benefit.

The second black action entails causing someone who has undertaken a positive action after careful deliberation to regret something which should not be regretted. The person is satisfied with his or her decision but we then say, "That is good but...," which causes them to have second thoughts and to regret what they have done. This is a black action because we have made them unhappy. Regretting a good action is non-virtuous, since it undermines the positive energy th. t has been created and discourages one from doing something worthwhile again in the future. On the other hand, regret when we have done something wrong is constructive because it decreases the negativity and discourages us from repeating the action.

For instance, a friend has become a monk and feels really happy about it. We say, "How nice that you've become a monk, but you know, when you go back to the West in robes, nobody will accept you, and if you stay in the East, you'll never be part of this community either." The friend might then begin to regret his decision to become ordained.

A Tibetan might tell one of his friends who has recently become a monk, "Of course, it's a very good thing to do but these days nobody has much respect for monks and you don't have to be ordained to practice." Needless to say, one doesn't take ordination to win others' respect but nobody likes to be an object of contempt. In the West there is a danger that people will not only fail to respect monks or nuns but actually look down on them as being unable to manage in normal life. People also sometimes say things like, "Well, the Buddha said you can give back your vows anytime." This is true and it's better to do so than to hold on to them just by the skin of one's teeth while indulging in all kinds of misconduct. However, it's wrong to take ordination with such a "come easy, go easy" attitude.

The third black action is to disparage a Bodhisattva out of anger. According to differing interpretations the object of disparagement is seen either as a Bodhisattva who has lost the altruistic intention or a Bodhisattva holding the Bodhisattva vow. Je Tsongkhapa indicates that it is simply a Bodhisattva with the altruistic intention. The disparagement may take different forms: it may be expressed as a general statement accusing the Bodhisattva of bad conduct, or the Bodhisattva may be accused of a particular action, or the action and where and when it was performed may be specified. The issue is not whether or not a negative action was performed but that the accusation is made out of anger with the intention to demean the Bodhisattva.

Anger is always destructive and particularly grave when directed at a Bodhisattva. Since we cannot know who is a Bodhisattva, it is best not to be angry with any living being. For one Bodhisattva to be angry with another is extremely grave, since anger is one of the Bodhisattva's most serious obstacles and is in direct conflict with the practice of love and compassion.

The fourth black action involves dishonesty with a bad motive. This refers to all forms of hypocritical and deceitful behavior for ignoble reasons.

Training in the Four White Actions

The four white actions are antidotes to the black ones. The first of these is never to lie to any living being with the intention to deceive, not as a joke nor even at the cost of our life. This counteracts the first black action of lying to our spiritual teacher and others.

The second is to maintain a sincere and honest attitude free from deceit and pretense towards all living beings. This counteracts the fourth black action of behaving deceitfully to others out of a bad intention. Deceit refers to hiding faults and weaknesses, while pretense refers particularly to giving the impression that we have qualities we do not possess.[13]

The third is to regard Bodhisattvas as our teachers and to praise them, which counteracts the third black action of disparaging them out of anger. The Buddha's disciple Mahakashyapa, who was renowned for his excellent ethical discipline and who led the spiritual community after the Buddha passed away, is said to have regarded all living beings as his teachers. The reason why our good actions don't yield much positive energy, which seems to decrease rather than increase, is because we disparage Bodhisattvas and our friends out of anger. It is wisest to cultivate pure perception of all beings. With those whom we like, we already do this because we tend to focus on their good qualities and over-look their faults.

Our praise of Bodhisattvas should be for qualities they actually possess and should only be voiced when a suitable opportunity arises, not foisted on unwilling ears. Bodhisattvas do not need our propaganda.

The fourth white action is to encourage those in our care not to follow the Lesser Vehicle but to seek complete enlightenment for the sake of all living beings. This counteracts the second black action of causing others to regret their good deeds. Though they may not respond by doing what we suggest, at least we will have tried to direct them towards complete enlightenment. Someone who really has the altruistic intention would never cause another person unhappiness by making them regret a good action.

Cultivating these four white actions insures that we will have the altruistic intention in future lives. By getting rid of pride which makes us feel superior, envy which makes us unable to bear others' success, miserliness which prevents us from giving and by rejoicing in the good qualities and success of others, we will never be separated from the altruistic intention. The *Cloud of Jewels Sutra*[14] tells us that we can also achieve this by constantly cultivating the altruistic intention while walking, standing, sitting and lying down and by making it precede everything we do.

We lose the promise we have made with regard to keeping the altruistic intention until we attain enlightenment by thinking that it's too much to have to work for all living beings or by resolving not to do anything more for a particular living being. However, even if this happens, we can restore our promise by arousing the altruistic intention again and by taking part in the ceremony of making the promise before our spiritual teacher. If this is not possible, we can do it before representations of enlightened body, speech and mind. Not arousing the altruistic intention three times a day and three times a night or not making offerings to create positive energy are faults but do not damage our commitment to maintain the altruistic intention.

If we have not taken the Bodhisattva vow, performing any of the black actions does not constitute the breach of a commitment. There are no downfalls involved, but through these black actions we create faults in our ethical discipline. Such faults should be purified by performing the *Confession Sutra*[15] or through other purificatory practices. If we hold the Bodhisattva vow, any of these four actions constitutes a transgression or downfall.

Maintaining our commitment to the aspiring altruistic intention and observing the precepts associated with it is a good preparation for the full ethical discipline of a Bodhisattva.

Chapter 7

The Ethical Discipline of Bodhisattvas

Once we have developed the aspiring altruistic intention, it is wise first to make a limited commitment by formally affirming our promise to maintain that aspiration until enlightenment and to observe the precepts associated with it. However, aspiration alone cannot bring about enlightenment. For this we must take the Bodhisattva vow and observe the ethical discipline of the Bodhisattva path, which is what past Bodhisattvas have done, what present Bodhisattvas do and what will be done by all future Bodhisattvas, since it is the only way to attain enlightenment. Taking the Bodhisattva vow lays the foundation for all Mahayana practice. It is essential for the Perfection Vehicle and also for every aspect of tantric practice.[1]

Bodhisattva conduct is extensively described in the *Avatamsaka Sutra*. Drawing on this Asanga wrote the *Bodhisattva Stages*,[2] which contains a chapter on the ethical discipline of Bodhisattvas. There are also various texts on the three sets of vows—the individual liberation vow, the Bodhisattva vow and the tantric vow—which describe how to safeguard them.[3] The longer version of the *Six Session Yoga*[4] lists the principal transgressions of the Bodhisattva vow and of the tantric vow.

Chandragomin's *Twenty Verses on the Bodhisattva Vow*[5] is based on Asanga's *Bodhisattva Stages*. The Bodhisattva vow is explained in terms of the preparation, the actual vow and the conclusion. It is vital first to understand what it is and to realize that we accumulate merit continuously, day and night, as long as we hold it. Those with a steadfast aspiration for enlightenment and a strong interest in the vow, who genuinely wish to hold it and are prepared to acknowledge and purify their faults, are ready to take the Bodhisattva vow.

Through living by this code of ethical discipline, we follow the Bodhisattva ideal and conform to the actual condition of an authentic Bodhisattva.[6] No matter how intelligent we are, if we fail to follow this code, we will never be true Bodhisattvas. It allows us to distinguish between what actions are and are not constructive. Understanding and remembering this, we then remain alert and vigilant. When we are about to do anything which is contrary to the vow, we conscientiously practice restraint. This basic procedure is a salient feature of the Buddhist approach and is not restricted to the ethical discipline of Bodhisattvas. It is not simply a question of whether or not we feel like doing something. The criterion is whether or not a specific action is appropriate. We try to refrain from actions which bring short-term happiness but long-term misery and to engage in those which bring long-term benefit, even though they may entail some immediate discomfort and difficulty. This may sound depressingly restrictive but in reality it is not.

The Bodhisattva vow has certain special beneficial features. The first of these is that it is conferred by someone else. When we are tempted to transgress the vow, remembering the spiritual teacher from whom we received it arouses a healthy sense of embarrassment which acts as a restraint. The second feature is that the vow fosters a pure state of mind. Our sense of self-esteem as a Bodhisattva and our dedication to this pure state of mind prevent us from creating transgressions that result from copying others' behavior or from trying to improve our personal reputation or livelihood. The third feature is that the vow can be restored. The fourth is that by respecting, cherishing and being mindful of it, our observance of the vow will not decline and we will not suffer from guilt or regret. To insure happiness and to avoid regret while holding the vow, we try not to damage it and quickly repair it when we do.

The Bodhisattva vow is generally taken from a spiritual teacher but when this is not possible, it may be taken before Buddhas and Bodhisattvas whose presence we invoke.

From the point of view of the holder, the ethical discipline of Bodhisattvas is divided into the Bodhisattva vow held by a lay person and the Bodhisattva vow held by an ordained person. Apart from the one day vow, there are five kinds of individual liberation vow which ordained people may hold and two that are held by lay people.[7]

It is not essential to hold any kind of individual liberation vow before taking the Bodhisattva vow but since we fulfill the necessary criteria and are capable of holding it, it is best to begin by taking on the individual liberation vow as part of the process of strengthening our commitment to practice the Buddha's teaching. Through this we create a special basis for holding the Bodhisattva vow. In the case of any of the individual liberation vows we make the commitment to keep that vow for as long as we live, whereas we promise to hold the Bodhisattva vow until we attain enlightenment. One continues to hold it after death if one has not given it up during one's lifetime.[8]

While it is possible to take individual liberation vows gradually, beginning with a one day vow, then the lay person's vow, followed by the novice monk's or nun's vow and finally the vow of a fully ordained monk or nun, each entailing a greater commitment, there is no such progressive way of taking the Bodhisattva vow. The preparation is to train in the precepts associated with the aspiring altruistic intention. Some texts advise that we should then think about certain aspects of Bodhisattva discipline. This has been misinterpreted as a way of partially taking the Bodhisattva vow.

The ethical discipline of Bodhisattvas falls into three categories: restraint from faulty action, accumulation of virtue and work for others.[9] This division into three has been compared to a tripartite division of vows associated with the Lesser Vehicle: individual liberation vows which are intended to stop the faulty behavior that springs from the disturbing emotions; vows of concentration which are intended to prevent the disturbing emotions from manifesting, and vows of no contamination whose purpose is to stop completely the continuity of the disturbing emotions.[10] It is, however, preferable to regard the three kinds of ethical discipline observed by Bodhisattvas as related to their two main tasks— of making themselves and others mature.

Restraint from wrong-doing and a rich accumulation of virtue help us to become mature and equip us to do what is beneficial for others. The ethical discipline of working for others helps them to gain spiritual maturity. How can we assist others to become mature and to find inner peace unless we become more mature and peaceful ourselves?

The disciplines of accumulating virtue and working for others can only be practiced successfully if they are founded on the ethical discipline of restraint from harmful actions. Anyone can practice this form of discipline. Those who hold any type of individual liberation vow practice such restraint by observing their lay person's or ordained person's vow. If we hold no vow of this kind, we practice restraint from ten harmful actions. These consist of three physical actions: killing, stealing and indulging in sexual misconduct. There are four harmful verbal activities: lying, using abusive or divisive language and wasting time on meaningless conversation. The three harmful mental activities in this context are covetousness, harmful thoughts and wrong views. Restraint from these ten activities is the basis for all Buddhist codes of conduct. Thus, even celestial beings and nagas who hold the Bodhisattva vow refrain from these ten harmful activities.

A lack of interest in such restraint is a major obstacle to holding the Bodhisattva vow, and without the Bodhisattva vow we cannot hold the tantric vow. Apart from a few minor points, the code of ethical discipline for lay and ordained practitioners of tantra is very similar. It is a grave mistake to see tantric empowerment as a carte blanche for undisciplined and unethical behavior.

Restraint from the ten harmful actions—even from just one of them—becomes a practice of those with the greatest capacity and a Bodhisattva activity when it is supported by the altruistic intention. The same restraint motivated by a wish for freedom from cyclic existence is a practice of those of intermediate capacity. If motivated by the wish for a good rebirth, it is a practice of persons whose capacity is limited. If we refrain from these actions because we consider them unwholesome, happiness will result, but from a Buddhist point of view this is not an authentic spiritual practice because the motivation does not encompass concerns beyond our present life. From this we see that a significant qualitative difference emerges, depending on the state of mind with which things are done.

New practitioners of the Bodhisattva vow focus on the development of restraint from harmful activity. Those on the later stages of the path of accumulation and on the path of preparation concentrate on the creation of virtue. Exalted Bodhisattvas devote themselves to activities which will further the well-being of others. However, all Bodhisattvas practice all three kinds of ethical discipline. To attain enlightenment we must make the Buddha's teachings ripen in our own mind stream, which is done through the creation of virtue. We must also help to make the teachings ripen and bear fruit in others, which is done by working for their well-being.

The ethical discipline of accumulating virtue cannot be practiced without refraining from harmful behavior. Virtue is accumulated in order to attain enlightenment for the sake of others. The practice itself consists of creating physical, verbal or mental virtue with this intention. These are the three salient features of a Bodhisattva's ethical discipline of creating virtue. A virtuous activity performed without the altruistic intention is not a Bodhisattva deed.

In order to accumulate virtue Bodhisattvas train in eight main areas and we can emulate them. The first is to strengthen our practice of the three kinds of training—in ethical discipline, concentration and wisdom—and to develop the three kinds of understanding derived from hearing, thinking and meditating. This creates virtue. Based on restraint from harmful conduct, which is the basis of all ethical discipline, we gain understanding derived from listening to teaching on sutras and commentaries dealing with the Bodhisattva way of life.[11] This leads to understanding derived from thinking and gaining certainty about what we have learned. The next step is the development of calm abiding and of special insight, which respectively constitute the training in meditative stabilization and the training in wisdom.

Ideally we should seek physical seclusion from a busy life and mental seclusion from disturbing emotions and from the constant flow of preoccupying thoughts. However, since contact with others can stimulate the growth of greater compassion and love, for Bodhisattvas mental seclusion from the disturbing emotions is more important than physical seclusion.

The second principal way of creating virtue is in relation to special fields or sources of merit which include those who have helped us, such as our parents, those with excellent qualities, for instance our spiritual teachers, and those who arouse our compassion such as the sick. We accumulate virtue not just by giving them material gifts but also by showing them respect. We do this in relation to our parents and teachers by not behaving casually in their presence and by, for example, greeting and receiving them warmly, inquiring after their well-being, offering them a good place to sit, rising to our feet when they enter a room and seeing them out when they leave. If we catch sight of them in the distance, even if they haven't noticed us, respectful behavior is appropriate.

All living beings should naturally be treated with respect, but our parents are singled out for mention here because they have given us our body. Our spiritual teachers are mentioned because they show us the way to happiness.

Nursing the sick, providing them with medicines and cheering them up, comforting and supporting those who are grief-stricken, and, in whatever ways we can, helping those who suffer are actions for which there are ample opportunities. However, they only become a Bodhisattva's creation of virtue if they are done with the altruistic intention to attain enlightenment for all living beings.

The third way of creating virtue is by developing a liking for good qualities and for those who have them. We remind ourselves to thank and praise those who teach us correctly about the true nature of reality and to appreciate and praise those who possess good qualities. When we hear others speak well of them, we should add our own praise without envy. Through this we can create as much virtue as those who possess the praiseworthy qualities. Training ourselves to rejoice in others' admirable accomplishments and abilities is an essential Bodhisattva activity.

The fourth source of virtue is patience. When we are harmed, two approaches are helpful. One is to think that through our own past actions we have set ourselves up as the target for this harm. Our present experience is the fruition of those actions. The other approach is to remember that the person who is inflicting the harm is dominated by the demon of disturbing emotions and is out of control. These emotions are not an integral part of their nature but something that temporarily overwhelms them and from which they can become free. For Bodhisattvas neither anger nor the wish for revenge are acceptable responses. On the contrary, they respond with love and the compassionate wish to help those who are harmful to throw off the burden of these disturbing emotions. Even if we are not yet Bodhisattvas, thinking in these ways can help us to remain calm in potentially explosive situations.

Prayers of dedication and aspiration are the fifth source of virtue.[12] We dedicate the merit from our physical, verbal and mental actions to our own enlightenment for the sake of others, to their peace, prosperity and happiness, and ultimately to their highest enlightenment. In this way we share our merit with them and the virtue we create will not end until they have all attained enlightenment themselves. We can steer the virtue in whatever direction we choose. Excellent prayers of aspiration may be found in the *Sutra of the Ten Stages* and in the *King of Prayers*.[13]

The sixth way to create merit is by making material offerings and offerings of our practice to the Three Jewels. There is never any shortage of things to offer, but what is lacking is our faith and willingness. We can offer the unowned natural beauty of rivers, lakes, forests, mountains, wildflowers and the sea as well as the creations of our imagination, but if we are in a position to make material offerings, we should not be too miserly to do so.

It is said that the offerings must "not be bad," meaning they should not have been acquired dishonestly nor should they be made with any ulterior motive. They should be "extensive," which means they should be generous and not niggardly, and the state of mind with which they are made should encompass the good of all sentient beings.

Living up the valley from Sera Monastery in central Tibet was Geshe Choktse, who had very few possessions. When he went to visit his spiritual master, Kyabje Trijang Dorje Chang, the junior tutor of His Holiness the fourteenth Dalai Lama, he would pick up the apricots lying on the ground under the fruit trees next to his home if he had nothing better to offer.

Once his benefactor gave him a warm meditation cloak. Since it was brand-new, he felt very happy and took it as an offering to Kyabje Trijang Rinpoche but Kyabje Rinpoche, knowing how poor he was, refused to accept it. Determined to offer it anyway, Gen Choktse put it over the mounting-block outside Kyabje Rinpoche's house.

I remember attending a teaching on *Offerings to the Spiritual Teacher*[14] given by Kyabje Trijang Rinpoche at Sera Monastery in South India. When explaining a particularly complex tantric practice, Kyabje Rinpoche remembered how Geshe Choktse had once confided that no matter how long he remained in meditative equipoise on emptiness, he only ever experienced bliss, whereas he had found this particular practice difficult. Geshe Choktse died in Wölka Chöling,[15] where Je Tsongkhapa had spent several years practicing very intensively.

The seventh way of creating virtue is by conscientiously directing our physical, verbal and mental activities away from non-virtue to virtue, such as the practice of the six perfections. And to create virtue in the eighth way the Bodhisattva is advised to train in all aspects of the path of accumulation. This means concentrating on constructive activities with mindfulness and mental alertness, which is impossible unless one can control the senses by not reacting with attachment to attractive objects, with aversion to unattractive objects and with confusion to neutral objects.

Our intake of food should be moderate, neither too little nor too much, since both extremes are an obstacle to virtuous conduct. Shantideva recommends that we should leave a third of our stomach empty. In addition to practicing during the day, the night should be divided into three parts and we should sleep only during the middle part. Much of our life is spent sleeping but this time need not be wasted because by falling asleep in a positive state of mind, the sleep which follows becomes a source of virtue.

We need good companions to encourage us and an inspiring spiritual teacher to guide us. If we cannot find such helpful companions and live far away from our spiritual teacher, we must be our own companion and mentor by recognizing faulty actions, remembering their disadvantages, applying counteractions and purifying them in front of representations of enlightened body, speech and mind or in the presence of Buddhas and Bodhisattvas whom we imagine before us.

Bodhisattvas on the great stage of the path of accumulation have constant access to the supreme emanation bodies of enlightened beings. Buddhas and Bodhisattvas are all around us but in ordinary form. When we behave negatively towards our spiritual companions, instead of hiding such actions, we should openly confess our wrong-doing and apologize. At present we tend to react defensively to any criticism of our actions and take an instant and intense dislike to the person who voiced it.

Since the individual liberation vow serves as a basis for the Bodhisattva vow and the tantric vow, it is a great mistake to see it as belonging exclusively to the Hinayana vehicle and as an obstacle to Mahayana practice. If Bodhisattvas who are monks or nuns hanker for past, present or future objects of desire and wish for what they have given up, their act of taking ordination becomes senseless. For lay Bodhisattvas non-attachment to past and present objects is not as important as non-attachment to future ones. This doesn't just mean a lack of attachment to the latest gadgetry. The creation of virtue now out of attachment to the sensual life one hopes to enjoy in future as a celestial being is a failure to observe the individual liberation vow, which is based upon a wish for freedom from all states of cyclic existence.

In brief, Bodhisattvas make effort to create fresh virtue by enhancing their practice of ethical discipline, concentration and wisdom and by developing the three kinds of understanding derived from hearing, thinking about and meditating on the teachings. They protect and safeguard their ethical discipline, particularly through patience, since virtue is undermined by anger. They enhance and strengthen it by rejoicing, dedicating their virtue to become a cause for others' well-being, and by making stainless prayers of aspiration. With the resolve to emulate them, we can begin training ourselves now to create virtue as they do.

When a significant store of virtue has been accumulated, the Bodhisattva concentrates on working for others. In his *Lamp for the Path to Enlightenment* Atisha stresses the importance of the different kinds of super-knowledge,[16] which allow one to know the dispositions, propensities and abilities of those one wants to help. Because of their developed intuition and insight those who have reached the Bodhisattva stages are able to work for others with assurance. Such Bodhisattvas do only what is appropriate, whereas at present we mostly rely on guess-work. The ethical discipline of working for the good of others entails turning away from every kind of action which does not accord with the principles of the Great Vehicle. There are eleven main ways in which Bodhisattvas work for the good of others.[17]

The first of these is to help others by assisting them in their activities, such as farming and business, provided this does not entail negativity. For instance a Bodhisattva may advise those who are trying to accumulate wealth and those who already have wealth on how to safeguard it, prevent it from declining, and on how to use it well. Conflict mediation is included in the assistance Bodhisattvas offer. They give help and friendship to the sick by caring for them or by making provision for their treatment and they assist travelers who are suffering from physical or mental problems to reach their destination. They learn to communicate with the deaf and teach them what is and is not constructive. These days of course there are motorized wheelchairs and many devices to help the disabled, but in the past the Bodhisattva might have had to carry the sick or disabled person.

The second way of working for others is to advise those who are confused about what means to employ. For instance, this might involve helping those who are suffering as a result of negative actions to understand what gives rise to suffering and what acts as a cause for happiness. On the other hand it may quite simply be a matter of giving them practical and clear advice on mundane matters and suggesting steps by which to proceed. To do this the Bodhisattva must be able to understand and assess situations correctly.

The third way by which Bodhisattvas work for others is by returning the help they have received in the past. Although we are not aware of it, all living beings have helped us in countless ways. Bodhisattvas behave in a friendly and welcoming manner to those whom they encounter, whether they know them or not. Even unasked, they provide or guide them to accommodation and food and do what they can to look after their needs.

The fourth way is to assist and protect those in fear. We all have rational justified fears but we also have many irrational fears. A Bodhisattva provides protection from danger and tries to alleviate fear wherever possible. Although we may not find ourselves launching dramatic rescue operations to save people's lives, there are many opportunities to save creatures from being burned, drowned, carried off by the wind or crushed by earth.

The fifth way is to console those in grief. People suffer bereavement when parted from parents, partners, children or spiritual teachers either through distance or death. Since it is rare to find affectionate friends who can be trusted, their loss is hard to bear. The death of a dog or cat is often a great loss to someone living alone. People also grieve when they lose their wealth or property through natural calamities, war or theft. Some lose it because they are careless, others by risking everything they have in the hope of gaining more. The Bodhisattva skillfully consoles and encourages the bereaved person to think about the teachings, particularly the impermanent nature of living beings, relationships and possessions. Often helping people to express their grief and listening attentively gives them consolation.

The sixth way is to help those in need. A Bodhisattva tries to provide whatever is required, such as food or shelter, companionship, good clothes and jewelry for those who feel they must keep up appearances, and even perfume and flowers for those who smell bad!

The seventh is to act as a support to those who are searching for someone on whom they can rely. Without self-interest, Bodhisattvas look after those who seek a spiritual teacher, providing them with material and spiritual sustenance, by, for instance, giving them instruction on how to develop mental stability.

The eighth is to help others according to their disposition and way of thinking. Bodhisattvas must understand the attitudes, aspirations and abilities of those they wish to help. Understanding their attitudes includes discerning which disturbing emotions predominate, whether the person tends towards wholesome or unwholesome activities, and to what extent their love and compassion have developed. Understanding their aspirations involves awareness of what people hope to accomplish and whether they wish to attain enlightenment, personal liberation, or a high rebirth. Their underlying disposition determines their capacity. This decides the nature of their practice which in turn determines the kind of result they can attain. For their help to be effective Bodhisattvas must be sensitive to all aspects of the other person.

What if our help makes that person unhappy? We should continue if it is useful in steering him or her away from harmful activities and if it will be of ultimate benefit. If our approach proves ineffective, we should try a new approach more in keeping with that person's temperament. When what we do is successful but our actions upset a third person, there is no need to stop, provided our intentions are good.

Many possible responses and situations are considered in this way. For example, it is recommended that people who are a "ball of anger" be left to cool down before we even try anything as positive as praising or apologizing to them. Since helping others and discussing matters that are important to them demands a certain degree of intimacy, we are encouraged not to cut ourselves off from others but to create friendships. On the other hand if we are too intrusive, our presence may stop them doing things they consider essential and they may come to resent us. We must therefore become skillful in sustaining relationships. In our enthusiasm to help we may be too trusting, which is a mistake when we do not know the other person well. People are not always what they appear to be. We should encourage others to do positive things within their capacity and discourage them from doing what is over-ambitious.

The ninth way is to support and encourage those engaged in excellent enterprises, such as cultivating faith, observing ethical discipline, studying the teachings, practicing generosity and developing wisdom. Ethical discipline and generosity are responsible for a good rebirth and sufficient resources. Wisdom is necessary for the attainment of liberation, since only it allows us to overcome the basic confusion which binds us to cyclic existence. However, wisdom comes only through listening to and studying the teachings, which one will not do unless one has interest and conviction in them.

The tenth way is to correct those who are not doing what they should and doing what they should not. It is misguided to tolerate and ignore their actions. When parents and teachers try to address such problems they often get upset, but a Bodhisattva remains clear and calm.

Whereas we can begin to practice these ten ways of helping others, we cannot perform the eleventh, the accomplishment of miraculous feats, until we have developed certain powers based on a high degree of meditative stabilization and not the less reliable kind of powers attained through the combination of substance and mantra.

The question arises as to whether there is a difference between compassion and pity. Compassion is always a positive emotion, whereas pity may be accompanied by feelings of superiority and condescension. We must guard against any attitude which devalues others and give importance to recognizing our own rather than others' faults. When others act in a negative way, we must try not to get upset nor to respond with anger, hostility or hatred. Instead, realizing that their behavior and the negative tendencies which underlie it are something temporary, we should try to help others get rid of them.

What if we have tried to help repeatedly without success? We should understand that everything does not depend on us. We can only help others if they want to be helped, and sometimes we have to acknowledge that we may not be able to help them in this life. Compassionate help for those in difficulty is, of course, good but the most useful thing we can do is to help them stand on their own feet. Resolving to work for the good of others just as Buddhas and Bodhisattvas do, we can begin to train ourselves now.

Chapter 8

Commentary on Chandragomin's *Twenty Verses on the Bodhisattva Vow*

In Sanskrit [the title of Chandragomin's text is] *Bodhisattvasaṃvara-viṃśaka*; in Tibetan, *Byang chub sems dpa'i sdom pa nyi shu pa* [and in English it is *The Twenty (Verses) on the Bodhisattva Vow*].

Homage to youthful Manjushri!

I.   Pay homage with reverence and offer what you can
      To the Buddhas and their children.
      This is the code of Bodhisattvas
      Existing everywhere, throughout time.

The verse indicates the preparations that are made for taking the Bodhisattva vow. When taking any category of the individual liberation vow, we are instructed first to make obeisance to our abbot and spiritual teacher but the need for offerings is not mentioned. Since the Bodhisattva vow is a vast undertaking for which we need much positive energy, we are instructed to imagine the presence of all Buddhas and Bodhisattvas of the past, present and future, to pay homage to them with faith inspired by their extraordinary abilities, and to make offerings to them according to our personal means.

II.   **Take that treasury of all merit,**
       With an excellent intention,
       From a spiritual teacher with ability
       Who observes the vow and is learned in it.

This verse deals with the actual taking of the vow and indicates what is to be taken, from whom and with what intention. The following verse describes the outcome or conclusion. There is no higher code of conduct than observance of the Bodhisattva vow, which is therefore unsurpassable. Since taking the vow is the result of an unparalleled wish to benefit all living beings, it creates supreme virtue. It is a treasury of limitless merit because it has the power to bring together all kinds of excellent and inexhaustible results. The merit gained by taking it far exceeds that created by taking any kind of individual liberation vow and this merit keeps growing until enlightenment is attained. Observing the vow acts as an effective antidote to faulty physical, verbal and mental actions towards others and is a supreme way of benefitting them.

The one who is to receive the vow must approach it with an excellent intention. Whether we are lay or ordained, we should wholeheartedly want to take the vow and have gained familiarity with the aspiring altruistic intention. Someone who wants to take the vow out of curiosity or interest but doesn't have the intention of sincerely observing it or training in the ethical discipline of a Bodhisattva is an unsuitable recipient.

In the case of the individual liberation vow it isn't customary to acquaint oneself beforehand with the discipline to be observed. However, if we wish to take the Bodhisattva vow, we should begin by finding out what the basic training entails and what constitutes faulty behavior. We should take it joyfully with a strong wish to hold the vow, not because we feel obliged to take it or because others have taken it, nor in a spirit of competitiveness.

The person from whom we take it may be younger, older, lay or ordained, but he or she should be someone we respect and who possesses spiritual qualities and insights superior to our own. If it is a peer, we are unlikely to feel sufficient respect. The person who confers the vow should have a good knowledge of the Mahayana scriptures, should be kindhearted and should not only have received the vow in the proper way but should actually be observing it. It should not be taken from just any scholarly person with knowledge of it, but only from one whose thoughts and deeds are pure in that he or she has a fervent regard for the vow and practices the six perfections.

We should not take the vow from those who are very attached to their property and who are miserly, greedy and discontented, because such behavior is antithetical to the practice of generosity. Nor should we take it from those who do not avoid downfalls and other transgressions of the vow,[1] since this is contrary to ethical discipline. The conduct of those who are easily upset and angered, bear grudges and seek revenge is in conflict with the practice of patience. Idleness, lack of interest in virtue and addiction to the pleasures of lazing about, sleeping and gossiping undermine enthusiastic effort, the active delight in virtue. Those who are easily distracted and cannot concentrate even for the time it takes to milk a cow are unable to practice meditative stabilization. Those whose understanding is limited through lack of knowledge about the nature of reality, and who fail to understand when it is explained or shrink from any discussion of it act in a manner that obstructs the development of true wisdom. The person from whom we take the vow should display none of these characteristics.

The spiritual teacher bestowing the vow should be able to confer it properly and have a good understanding of the ceremony. Those who hope to receive the vow should show various tokens of respect and make offerings before receiving it.[2] They prepare the place where the vow will be given by cleaning and decorating it and by setting up representations of the body, speech and mind of enlightened beings in front of which they arrange these offerings. They imagine themselves to be in the presence of Buddhas and Bodhisattvas, and they take to mind their many excellent qualities. Seeing the spiritual teacher as an enlightened being, they invite him or her to sit on the throne that has been prepared and with strong faith they then take heartfelt refuge, arouse the altruistic intention and perform the seven-part practice according to Shantideva's *Way of the Bodhisattva* or according to *The King of Prayers, the Prayer of Noble Conduct* [see Appendix 2] in order to purify themselves and to create merit.

They promise to free all living beings from suffering and to help them reach the state of non-abiding nirvana.[3] For this purpose they make the commitment to observe the vow, following in the footsteps of all Bodhisattvas of the past, doing what all future Bodhisattvas will do and what all present Bodhisattvas of the ten directions are engaged in doing.

III.   Then, because it is definite,[4]
         Buddhas and their children
         With their virtuous hearts will always
         Consider you their beloved child.

As a natural consequence of the recipient's definite commitment to the vow and through the powerful virtue of taking it, the earth trembles and the seats of Buddhas and Bodhisattvas shake. When they look for the cause, they see the one who has taken the vow, where and from whom. The Buddhas then rejoice at the birth of a precious child and the Bodhisattvas at the birth of a beloved sibling. With their virtuous hearts they pray that the new Bodhisattva may always meet with good fortune and never with harm, and that he or she will be able to create virtue continuously until enlightenment.

These verses have described how to prepare for the vow, the actual ceremony of taking the vow for the first time and the conclusion. Now Chandragomin tells us, first in general and then in particular, how to protect the vow.

IV.   For others and also for yourself,
       Do what is useful even if painful,
       And what is both useful and pleasurable,
       Not what gives pleasure but is of no use.

Motivated by compassion the Bodhisattva is intent on helping living beings find happiness and avoid suffering. A Bodhisattva who misses opportunities to make others happy and who ignores their unhappiness and suffering is at fault. Working for others takes much enthusiastic effort, for which accumulation of positive energy and purification of negativity are necessary. A Bodhisattva who neglects to do this is also at fault.

Here "useful" refers to that which will benefit one in future lives, while "pleasurable" refers to agreeable feelings now. If something is ultimately beneficial and also pleasurable now, it is certainly worth doing. If it is neither beneficial in the long run nor pleasurable now, it is definitely not worth doing. If it is painful now but beneficial in the long run, such as refraining from transgressions of the Bodhisattva vow, it is worth persevering. If it is pleasurable now, like sexual misconduct, but ultimately harms us and others, it should not be done. We must be prepared to put up with small difficulties in order to prevent much greater ones and to sacrifice small pleasures for the sake of lasting happiness. These are useful general guidelines and show how essential it is to be fully conscious of our actions.

We need the help of a spiritual teacher with good knowledge and experience of the teachings on the Bodhisattva way of life in order to protect our Bodhisattva vow from damage. Having received and understood the necessary instructions, we should put them into practice by first learning what constitute the eighteen major and forty-six minor transgressions and by then trying to avoid them.

Without sound ethical discipline even the practice of tantra will not yield the desired fruit. Scrupulousness regarding ethical discipline means taking care to avoid faults and purifying them when they occur. We can benefit from doing this even now because it protects us from unhappiness, guilt and regret. Our disciplined physical and verbal activity wins others' respect and makes it easy for them to create a relationship with us.

Most people are quite confused about what is and is not constructive and need to establish clear criteria. The teachings, which come to us as part of a living tradition and bring with them the blessings of the great teachers of the past, provide us with clear criteria. Reading the biographies of past practitioners can increase our faith and aspiration. If it makes us more careful of our conduct and more enthusiastic about even small positive actions, we are experiencing the blessings of these great teachers. Our inner transformation is evidence of their blessings.

Who can create a transgression? Those who are deranged, those who are overwhelmed by grief and those who have not taken the vow cannot create a transgression. A transgression can be created only by someone who is in a normal state of mind and who has both taken and received the Bodhisattva vow and still holds it.

In the case of the individual liberation vow there are five kinds of transgressions, but there are only two kinds of transgressions of the Bodhisattva vow: basic downfalls and faulty actions.[5] Of the eighteen basic downfalls or major transgressions of the Bodhisattva vow, two cause us to lose it at once: giving up the altruistic intention and holding wrong views. In the case of the other sixteen, we lose the vow only if these transgressions are accompanied by the four binding factors.

V.   Coming from strong disturbing emotions,
      They are what destroy the vow.
      All four of their transgressions
      Are considered to be like defeats.

The list of transgressions begins with a set of four basic
downfalls for Bodhisattvas holding the vow. These are
praising oneself or belittling others; withholding teachings
or wealth; not accepting an apology or striking another;
and giving up the Great Vehicle or giving counterfeit teachings. Eight different negative actions are involved but they
are classed as four groups of two because each group shares
the same motivation: attachment, miserliness, harmful intent and confusion, respectively.

These are considered to be like the defeats of the individual liberation vow inasmuch as they make us lose the
Bodhisattva vow if they come from strong disturbing emotions, namely if they are done with all four of the binding
factors. However, these actions are not like defeats in all re-
spects, because even if we lose the Bodhisattva vow in this
way, we can take it again, whereas if we create a defeat of
the individual liberation vow, the vow becomes as useless
as a burnt seed and cannot be taken again in this life.[6]

The four binding factors together are called "great contamination."[7] They are not wanting to stop but wishing to repeat
the action, lacking shame and decency, taking joy and delight
in the action, and seeing nothing wrong with the action.[8] Of
these, two indicate that certain vital attitudes are lacking.
Unless we consider what we are doing as wrong, we won't
feel any shame or embarrassment about it, and normally the
reason why we don't see the action as negative is because we
are attracted to it and want to do it. Even if we realize it is
wrong, we may still enjoy doing it and want to repeat it.

When great contamination in the form of all four factors
accompanies these transgressions, they become basic downfalls and we lose the vow. Of the four binding factors, seeing nothing wrong with the action is worst. If it alone is
present, or it and one or two other factors are present, the

transgression is accompanied by moderate contamination. If any of the factors excluding the fourth is present, the transgression is accompanied by minor contamination. Transgressions accompanied by moderate and minor contamination are not actual downfalls and do not make us lose the vow, but they belong to the category of downfalls. In some texts these are listed as a third kind of transgression of the Bodhisattva vow but, as mentioned above, there are actually only two kinds of transgressions—downfalls and faulty actions.

These binding factors operate during the preparation for or during the actual creation of the transgression but they do not need to be present throughout the action until the conclusion. A basic downfall, for instance, can be created, even if by the end of the action one feels regret.

VI.   With attachment to reward, respect and service,
        Praising oneself or disparaging others;
        Out of miserliness not giving teaching
        Or wealth to the suffering and unprotected.

Reward refers to material gain such as food, clothing, a place to live and wealth or property of various kinds. The words *respect* and *service*[9] refer to an elevated status and special treatment. We are not motivated by attachment if we seek material benefits or respect because we wish to create an opportunity to make offerings to the Three Jewels or are moved by compassion to help others who are in need. Attachment here implies that we have a selfish motivation for wanting the rewards or respect. Many people cannot bear to sit in any but the best seats or wear any but the smartest clothes!

The person disparaged or belittled is someone other than oneself who by consensus is considered worthy of respect because he or she possesses good qualities. The praise of oneself or disparagement of the other must actually be voiced to another human being and be understood. The commentaries mention that the utterance is made to "a being of the same species" thereby emphasizing that the remark must be understood. If the reward we seek is a part of the property or wealth we share with others and, for instance, we are trying to win exclusive ownership of it, the act is negative but not the downfall referred to here. We may, of course, also be seeking special treatment by those with whom we share property or resources.

The one who is refused teachings or wealth is a suffering and friendless person in need of help, who has no one else to turn to and whose request is genuine and not just made to test our generosity. The person may ask for material goods or spiritual instruction. It is not negative to refuse requests for unsuitable things such as poison or weapons, nor is it negative if Bodhisattvas refuse to give things or pass on knowledge that they do not possess. However, if Bodhisattvas withhold what is in their possession out of miserliness, they create a transgression.

VII.   Not heeding the confession of others;
       Striking them in anger;
       Rejecting the Great Vehicle;
       Giving a counterfeit of the excellent teachings.

The other person knows he or she has done something wrong, feels genuinely sorry and makes a clear apology or confession. We understand it but, out of anger, do not want to forgive and intentionally refuse to accept the apology.

Out of anger we may say something unpleasant. Despite venting our anger in this way, it does not subside but intensifies and with aggressive resentment we strike the other person. The object of the attack is someone of the same species as the one who holds the vow. Although only striking is mentioned, other kinds of physical harm such as imprisonment, mutilation, bondage or taking the life of another human being are included here.

The "excellent teachings" refers to Mahayana scriptures. Rejecting them means to disparage them or to assert that they are not the authentic teachings of the Buddha. For instance, we may find the subject-matter of the Perfection of

Wisdom sutras, which explain the profound and extensive paths of practice, too complex to understand or we may not like what they say and therefore reject them, claiming they are not the Buddha's words.

Counterfeit teachings are those which do not accord with the Buddha's. We create this fault if we like such teachings, engage in practicing them, promulgate them and encourage others to practice them.

When we have the opportunity to receive and think about teachings relating to the complete paths and stages to enlightenment, beginning with the cultivation of a relationship with a qualified spiritual teacher, it is a great mistake to confine ourselves to a limited practice like meditation on the energy channels, winds and drops.[10] Though the teachings we practice may be authentic, we do ourselves a disservice through this. How does breathing meditation become a virtuous practice, unless it is supported by a positive motivation? Breathing is no more virtuous than getting up and sitting down, doing which repeatedly can serve as a form of exercise. It is vital that any practice we do should be a complete one.

The great master Atisha held all three kinds of vows. He said that he had never transgressed the individual liberation vow, that he had created some faults in relation to the Bodhisattva vow and many many faults, like pouring rain, with regard to the tantric vow. However, he also mentioned that he had never spent a single day without purifying any fault he had created.

Although a number of factors must be present to create a basic downfall, it can happen more easily than the creation of a defeat of the individual liberation vow. For instance, sexual intercourse out of desire creates a defeat of the individual liberation vow, but desire for reward and respect is enough to create a transgression of the Bodhisattva vow. Similarly, taking others' wealth is a defeat of the individual liberation vow, whereas refusing to give what one owns out of miserliness is a transgression of the

Bodhisattva vow. Killing a human being creates a defeat of the individual liberation vow, while refusing to accept a sincere apology or inflicting bodily harm out of anger is a transgression of the Bodhisattva vow. Pretending to possess realizations one doesn't have constitutes a defeat of the individual liberation vow, but simply withholding teachings out of miserliness is a transgression of the Bodhisattva vow.

While the individual liberation vow cannot be taken again, once a defeat has been created, the Bodhisattva vow can fortunately be renewed, but nevertheless we shouldn't think that since it can be taken again, losing the Bodhisattva vow is of no consequence. It is in fact a more serious matter than creating a defeat of the individual liberation vow. Creating a basic downfall is an obstacle to reaching the Bodhisattva stages—one will not become an exalted Bodhisattva in this life nor accumulate the positive energy necessary to become an exalted Bodhisattva.

Many of us have taken the Bodhisattva vow but do we actually hold it or not? Ideally to hold the Bodhisattva vow our altruistic intention should have developed to such an extent that it arises effortlessly and the spiritual teacher who bestows the vow should have the qualities already described. His Holiness the Dalai Lama invests great energy in trying to arouse some feeling in us when he confers the Bodhisattva vow, so that at least for a few moments we may have some form of altruistic intention. He always says that if we don't feel anything, to whom do the words "I, the Bodhisattva ..." refer when we make the promise? By encouraging us so forcefully to think about these matters, he makes us rich in virtue. He then encourages us to dedicate that virtue to act as a cause not just for our own personal well-being but for the peace and happiness of all, thereby making it inexhaustible.

The more capable we are of rising to the occasion, the more we receive. For example, during an empowerment it is essential to follow the instructions regarding what to visualize and to participate fully while the empowerment is being conferred, otherwise we do not really receive it. Being present without doing this is of some value because it implants good imprints, but we do not attend empowerments merely as spectators. If we are actively taking part, our attention will be so intense that we may feel quite exhausted by the end. People often remark what good fortune it is to receive a particular empowerment, but it is really only good fortune if we claim our rightful share of what is being offered to us.

VIII.   **The vow should be taken again.**
   Confess moderate contamination to three,
   And to one. The rest, with and without disturbing emotions,
   Are similarly [confessed in] one's own mind.

When any of the first four basic downfalls, comprising the eight actions mentioned above, has been created, the vow is lost and must be taken again. When a transgression accompanied by moderate contamination has been created, it should be confessed in the presence of three or more people, and in the case of minor contamination it should be confessed to one or more persons. The forty-six minor transgressions, called faulty actions, need not be confessed publicly but must be acknowledged in one's own mind.[11]

The fourteen remaining basic downfalls are supplemented from the fourth chapter of Shantideva's *Compendium of Training*[12] which says:

   Robbing what belongs to the Three Jewels
   Is a downfall likened to a defeat.
   Rejecting the excellent teachings
   Is named as the second by the Subduer.

The fifth downfall, listed as the first in *The Compendium*, is robbing the Three Jewels of what belongs to them. The jewel of enlightened beings in this context refers not only to enlightened beings but also to their images and stupas. The jewel of the teachings, which normally refers to the true cessation of suffering and to true paths of insight, here refers to texts containing the teachings. The jewel of the spiritual community, usually consisting of exalted beings, here refers to any group of four or more ordained persons.

Their belongings are offerings made to them, materials for constructing statues such as precious metals or jewels, the paper, ink, wood blocks and other resources for printing texts, cloth to make book covers for them, and places where statues, texts and the spiritual community are housed. If, knowing that these belong to the Three Jewels, we willfully take them by stealth or force and then feel satisfied that we have acquired what we sought, we have created this transgression.

For example, if we are in charge of regilding a statue and keep some of the gold offered for this purpose or if we keep for personal use silk offered for wrapping texts, we create this transgression. Even if all the factors that make it a downfall are not present, the action remains negative.

The sixth downfall, mentioned as the second in *The Compendium*, is to reject the excellent teachings. The teachings referred to contain a complete explanation of the paths relevant to a particular vehicle, for instance explaining both the profound and extensive aspects of Bodhisattva practice in the case of the Perfection Vehicle; completely explaining the four noble truths in the case of the Hearer Vehicle; fully explaining the twelve links of dependent arising in the case of the Solitary Realizer Vehicle. The downfall involves disparaging any such teachings and denying that they are authentic teachings of the Buddha. The rejection of a teaching containing only a partial explanation of the above-mentioned topics does not constitute a downfall but is nonetheless a grave negative action.

The Compendium says:

> The third is to seize the robes,
> Strike or put in prison,
> Demote from ordination or deprive of life
> Even a monk with faulty discipline.

The seventh downfall, listed as the third in *The Compendium*, is to seize the robes of an ordained person. This person's observance of ethical discipline may be good or faulty. The robes are taken by force and, with the intention to cause harm, the person is expelled from the monastic community and made to enter lay life. The action is underlain by violence.

If someone is expelled from the monastic community because he or she could lead a more constructive life as a lay person and the action is performed out of compassion, it does not create a fault. Nagarjuna is said to have expelled tens of thousands of monks and in recent times in Tibet Kyabje Ling Rinpoche[13] expelled quite a few monks from Gyütö Tantric College[14] while he held a position of authority there. This was for the good of the monastic community, for the flourishing of the teachings and to prevent negative actions.

Striking, imprisoning, causing bodily injury to, or taking the life of such an ordained person in this context constitute the third downfall mentioned in Asanga's *Bodhisattva Stages* and in Chandragomin's *Twenty Verses*, "Striking them in anger."

From *The Compendium*:

> Performing the five heinous actions,[15]
> Holding wrong views,
> Also destroying villages and so forth
> Were said to be basic downfalls by the Subduer.

The eighth downfall, mentioned as the fourth in *The Compendium*, concerns five very serious negative actions: patricide, matricide, killing a Foe Destroyer, causing schism in the spiritual community and drawing blood from an enlightened being with the intention to harm. Killing one's father or mother is particularly grave because our parents have given us life and in most cases they have done a great deal for us. A Foe Destroyer possesses outstanding qualities, having completely overcome all disturbing emotions. The death of such a person is a loss to the world. Causing schism in the spiritual community has a detrimental effect not only on the community but on the whole surrounding area. There is no need to mention the gravity of intentionally harming an enlightened being.

The ninth downfall, the fifth in *The Compendium*, concerns wrong views, which in this context refer to a belief that there is no connection between actions and their effects and that there are no past and future lives. The former makes it impossible for us fully to practice non-violence as described by the Buddha. Some interpretations state that this downfall entails performing one of the ten harmful actions or encouraging others to do so as a result of holding wrong views. This is incorrect, since the basic downfall occurs as soon as the wrong view is held, even in the absence of the binding factors.

The tenth downfall, the sixth in *The Compendium*, involves the destruction of places such as villages, towns, regions and countries. The destruction of living beings belongs to the third downfall listed in Asanga's *Bodhisattva Stages* and in Chandragomin's *Twenty Verses*, "Striking them in anger," which includes all forms of physical violence. The destruction of their property belongs to the first downfall listed in *The Compendium*, "Robbing what belongs to the Three Jewels," or to the thirteenth, "Having practitioners of virtue fined and accepting what was given and donated to the Three Jewels."

The Compendium says:

> Speaking about emptiness to a living being
> Whose mind has not been prepared;
> Making those engaged in [attaining] Buddhahood
> Turn away from complete enlightenment;
> After they have given up individual liberation,
> Involving them in the Great Vehicle.
> Saying and convincing them that the Learners' Vehicle
> Cannot eliminate attachment and so forth;
> Also making them enter [the Great Vehicle].

The eleventh downfall, the seventh according to *The Compendium*, is to explain emptiness to those whose minds are unprepared. This downfall is created in relation to those with the altruistic intention who have not made a careful study of the nature of reality. When emptiness is explained to them, they feel afraid and misunderstand it to mean that nothing exists. As a result they may reject the teachings of the Great Vehicle and instead choose to follow those of the Lesser Vehicle. This does not apply to people who have never thought about reality, since an explanation of emptiness would mean very little to them and would not cause fear. The person who creates this transgression has not made any effort to discover whether the recipient of the explanation is properly prepared or not. If an assessment was made and misjudgment occurred, the downfall is not created.

The twelfth downfall, the eighth according to *The Compendium*, is to turn someone away from complete enlightenment. This downfall occurs in relation to practitioners of the Great Vehicle who, for instance, feel overwhelmed by the vastness of the practices that must be done to attain Buddhahood. The downfall is created by telling them that they would find the six perfections too difficult to practice and would not be capable of attaining complete enlightenment, thereby persuading them that it would be much better and quicker to aim simply for personal liberation from cyclic existence.

The thirteenth downfall, listed as the ninth in *The Compendium*, is to persuade someone who is observing the individual liberation vow well to give it up in favor of Mahayana practices, by saying, for example, that the latter can rid one of every kind of fault, or that observance of the higher kinds of vow, such as the Bodhisattva or tantric vow, is of much greater significance than observance of the individual liberation vow.

The fourteenth downfall, the tenth according to *The Compendium*, concerns disparaging the paths of Hearers and

Solitary Realizers, referred to as the Learners' Vehicle.[16] If the other person believes us when we say that disturbing emotions like attachment cannot be eliminated by practicing these paths, we have created this downfall. While the sixth downfall, listed as the second in *The Compendium*, "Rejecting the excellent teachings," involves a rejection of the scriptural teachings of the Lesser Vehicle, this one consists of persuading others to reject these teachings from the point of view of the realizations which they produce.[17] This downfall is created even if the person dissuaded from practicing the teachings of the Learners' Vehicle does not adopt the practices of the Great Vehicle.

The Compendium says:

> Speaking about one's own good qualities
> And disparaging others for reward, respect
> And for the sake of verses.
> Saying what is false [such as]
> "I can tolerate the profound."

The eleventh downfall in *The Compendium* is included in the first of the downfalls enumerated in Asanga's *Bodhisattva Stages* and in Chandragomin's text: "Praising oneself or belittling others." The explanation presented in *The Compendium* is a narrower interpretation of the downfall than that found in Asanga's text and should therefore be included within the broader one. *The Compendium* explains that the person who creates this downfall is actually attached to reward or respect but when studying or teaching claims to be quite uninterested in such things. He or she implies that someone else is motivated by such attachments, thereby disparaging a person in whom a listener may have faith. Not only is this done out of attachment to gaining reward or respect but also out of envy. *The Compendium* uses the phrase "And for the sake of verses."[18] This probably refers to the wish to be praised in verse. Je Tsongkhapa glosses it as meaning a wish for renown.

The fifteenth downfall, listed as the twelfth in *The Compendium*, consists of consciously telling a lie with regard to one's realizations. If in fact we haven't gained understanding of emptiness but teach another person about it and tell them, "If you meditate on what I have taught you, you'll gain a direct experience of emptiness like me!" we create this transgression. Here the subject-matter of the lie is restricted to the profound nature of reality. In the case of the individual liberation vow, a defeat is created not only through this kind of lie but also if we claim to have achieved a calmly abiding mind, special insight or certain clairvoyant powers associated with the path, when we know this to be untrue. If we genuinely but wrongly think we have achieved such insights, the downfall or defeat is not created.

The Compendium says:

> Having practitioners of virtue fined,
> And accepting what was given
> And donated to the Three Jewels.
> Making them give up calm abiding
> And giving to those who perform recitation
> The resources of practitioners of concentration—
> These are the basic downfalls
> Which are causes for the hell realms of living beings.
> They should be confessed in dream
> Kneeling before Exalted Essence of Space.

The sixteenth downfall, listed as the thirteenth in *The Compendium*, involves taking what belongs to the Three Jewels by, for instance, initiating action to fine a practitioner of virtue and accepting money or goods acquired in this way. The downfall is not about stopping that person's practice of virtue, which is included in the seventh downfall, listed as the third in *The Compendium*: "Taking away the robes of the ordained and expelling them." It is also not about taking away their property, which is included in the fifth downfall, listed as the first in *The Compendium*: "Robbing the Three Jewels of what belongs to them." In general it is negative to make use of things that have been stolen or even forcibly acquired or confiscated, whether or not the law allows for the latter.

The seventeenth downfall, the fourteenth according to *The Compendium*, is to follow bad discipline by depriving an ordinary person practicing concentration of resources and giving these to someone engaged in the recitation of texts. By doing this we disrupt the meditator's practice and the state of mind conducive to the cultivation of calm abiding or special insight, cause trouble and arouse disturbing emotions.

Creating any of these basic downfalls is a great loss for Bodhisattvas who have entered the Mahayana paths, since it undermines the virtue they have accumulated and means that they will fall from Mahayana states of happiness as celestial beings and humans into bad rebirths. They will be forced to remain for a long time within cyclic existence and will be separated from spiritual teachers.

In his *Way of the Bodhisattva* Shantideva reminds us that when we have taken the Bodhisattva vow, it is essential to understand how many possible transgressions there are, what they consist of and how to purify them. He says:

> The training you will find described
> Within the sutras. Therefore read and study them.
> *The Sutra of the Essence of Sky*—[19]
> This is the text that should be studied first.

To purify the negativity we have accumulated we should visualize the Bodhisattva Akashagarbha, Essence of Sky or Space,[20] before us, confess the downfall and apply the four counteractions.[21] The words "in dream" here may be taken literally but can also refer to imagining or visualizing the Bodhisattva.[22] Transgressions involving middling and minor contamination should be purified in the same way. However, confession does not restore the vow that was lost by creating a basic downfall. In this case the vow must be taken again. When middling or minor contamination are present, the vow is restored by confessing before three people and one person respectively in accordance with the prescribed ritual.[23]

The eighteenth downfall, that of giving up the altruistic intention, is taken from the *Wise in Skillful Means Sutra*.[24] This sutra explains that a Bodhisattva observing the discipline prescribed by the individual liberation vow, who spends a hundred or even a thousand aeons eating only roots and fruits and who practices forbearance, whether others speak pleasantly or unpleasantly, would create a very grave downfall if, out of self-interest, he or she were to develop the wish to attain the enlightenment of a Hearer or Solitary Realizer. Without purifying this transgression the Bodhisattva would not be able to attain Buddhahood.

Since the person who creates this downfall is a Bodhisattva who holds the Bodhisattva vow, this refers to giving up the aspiring altruistic intention. During the first moment of giving up that intention, the Bodhisattva still holds the vow but loses it in the second. The same applies in the case of developing a wrong view.

The sutra explains what it means to be wise in skillful means. By giving just a mouthful of food Bodhisattvas can nourish all living beings because of their intention to benefit all and their wish for the merit they create to act as a cause for universal happiness. When they rejoice in the good done by others, they dedicate even the positive energy this creates to the well-being of all.

It is possible to give back the individual liberation vow one has taken. When this is done, the positive energy one creates while holding it ceases but no negativity is entailed. However, giving back the Bodhisattva vow is considered very negative, since one is rescinding the promise made to attain enlightenment exclusively for the sake of helping living beings.

If we take and hold the vow without creating any of the basic downfalls and if we do not give it back nor give up the aspiring altruistic intention, we still retain the vow when we die. Then, wherever we take birth, we will have the natural tendency to do what is positive and to avoid whatever conflicts with the vow. We will have a kindhearted nature and a natural interest in spiritual growth and transformation. Meeting with a spiritual teacher will awaken in us the imprints left by our observance of the vow.

Chandragomin's *Twenty Verses* continues with the forty-six transgressions which are faulty actions and which may be created by those who hold the vow and who are in a sane state. These faulty actions may or may not be accompanied by disturbing emotions.[25]

IX.   Not offering the three to the Three Jewels;
      Following thoughts of desire;
      Not respecting one's seniors;
      Giving no answer to questions.

1. "Not offering the three to the Three Jewels": Here the jewel of the Buddhas is identified as enlightened beings, their images and stupas representing their minds. The texts containing the teachings represent the jewel of the teachings. The spiritual community is identified in the narrow sense of exalted beings, namely those who have reached the path of seeing and beyond.

Not making offerings to the Three Jewels by physical acts of homage, through praise and by mental acts of faith undermines primarily the practice of material generosity. If we make even one prostration to an image of the Buddha, we have not created this faulty action. If we do not make offerings out of spite, anger or other such feelings, the action is accompanied by disturbing emotions. If we simply forget, it is not.

When the faulty actions which follow are done out of laziness, defined as a lack of interest in virtue, or because of lethargy, the feeling that we can't be bothered, they are said to have been created without the presence of disturbing attitudes or emotions, although strictly speaking laziness and lethargy are actually classed as disturbing attitudes, albeit somewhat less serious ones. In this case, however, since making extensive offerings to the Three Jewels is an essential Bodhisattva practice, laziness counts as a disturbing emotion. If we make a concerted effort to stop a disturbing emotion but do not succeed, the action we perform is negative and faulty but it does not constitute a transgression.

2. "Following thoughts of desire" refers to allowing greedy thoughts, discontentment, dissatisfaction and attachment to reward and respect to occupy our mind. If we do so, we fail to counteract miserliness, which is antithetical to the practice of generosity. This faulty action consists of making no effort to stop such thoughts and is never created without disturbing emotions. It conflicts with the ethical discipline of practicing restraint from faulty action because our desire and attachment often cause us to act in ways which harm us and others. If we recognize that such thoughts are counterproductive and genuinely try to stop them again and again by applying antidotes but they nevertheless keep coming, we do not create this transgression but our actions are not without fault.

3. "Not showing respect to seniors": The person to whom respect is not shown is someone who is our senior in holding the Bodhisattva vow, who possesses admirable qualities, is trustworthy and warrants respect. If respect is withheld out of envy or competitiveness the faulty action is performed with disturbing emotions. The action may also be performed out of laziness. It conflicts with the generosity of giving protection because if we fail to show deference towards those who are our seniors, our appearance and conduct do not inspire confidence and trust and the other person may feel threatened and vulnerable.

No fault is involved if we are too sick or weak to rise and show respect. Nor is there any fault if the person who is our senior is arrogant or angry and we remain seated out of a wish to help them correct this behavior. We may also remain seated if rising would upset others or disturb them during teachings.

4. "Giving no answer to questions": The question is sincere and asked in a pleasant way. If out of anger we give a dishonest answer or answer correctly but in an unpleasant way, the faulty action is performed with disturbing emotions. It may also be performed out of laziness. If someone wishes to wake us from sleep and does so by asking a question which we fail to answer properly on waking, no fault is created because the question was used merely as an expedient. If we are sick or weak, wish to teach, are involved in a discussion or in a conversation intended to make someone else happy or are listening to teaching, no fault is created by not answering the question. Like the previous faulty action, this transgression is also contrary to the generosity of giving protection, since it is a Bodhisattva's duty to protect others' minds.

X.   Not accepting invitations;
       Not taking such things as gold;
       Not giving to those who seek teaching;
       Disdaining the immoral.

5. By "not accepting invitations" we deprive others of the opportunity to practice generosity. The invitation may be individual and private or to a gathering in a temple to receive food, money or clothes. Refusing to participate out of pride or anger means the faulty action is created with disturbing emotions. It may also be created out of laziness or lethargy. If we are weak or sick, have previously been invited elsewhere or are involved in the intensive practice of virtue, no fault is created by not attending.

The place to which we have been invited may be too distant, too difficult or too dangerous to reach, in which case there is no fault in not attending. If we suspect that we will be humiliated, it is permissible to refuse the invitation. It is also valid to refuse if we are receiving a new teaching, hearing accounts and information we have not heard before, protecting the mind of another or if the invitation goes against the code of discipline for the ordained. This code, for instance, delineates the situations in which alms may and may not be accepted.

6. "Not taking such things as gold," silver, precious and semi-precious stones out of pride, anger or the wish to hurt is a faulty action motivated by disturbing emotions. We may also refuse these gifts out of laziness and lethargy. No fault is created by refusing to accept what is given if we think we will grow attached to it, suspect that the benefactor has made a mistake and really intended to give the gift to someone else, that he or she did not really mean to give this particular thing, may later regret giving it, or will become poor as a result of making lavish gifts. We may also refuse if we think what is being given belongs to the Three Jewels, to someone else or has been stolen. We may refuse if we think the donor will be punished for giving the gift or we for receiving it.

This faulty action and the previous one are both contrary to the ethical discipline of working for others, which involves creating opportunities for others to accumulate positive energy.

7. "Not giving to those who seek teaching" may occur with or without the presence of disturbing emotions. There is no fault if we are sick, too weak or incapable of giving the teaching requested. We may refuse if the request has been made simply to create an opportunity to argue, if the person who makes the request is mentally disrespectful or speaks and acts in an ill-mannered way. Teaching should never be given unrequested and even when requested only after a proper examination of the recipient has been made to establish whether the teaching is suitable for that person. If he or she is unready for it, too unintelligent to understand the profound and extensive practices correctly or likely to misinterpret what is said and to form wrong views, the teaching

may be refused. We may attempt to explain everything clearly but if we discover that the person persists in their preconceptions, there is no need to continue. If we suspect that the other is capable of understanding the teaching but may misuse it, there is also no fault in refusing to teach.

These first seven faulty actions go against the ethical discipline of creating virtue and specifically against practice of the perfection of giving. The second, "following thoughts of desire," consists of doing something we shouldn't do, while the others consist of not doing what we should do. There are certain times and certain situations when we are more likely to perform these faulty actions. Knowing this, it is wise to take special care when those circumstances arise.

We cannot train ourselves in giving, ethical discipline, patience and so forth unless we guard our mind from influence by the disturbing emotions. If we don't tame our own mind, how can we hope to help others tame their minds? The body is relatively easy to control but the mind is not and needs to be disciplined and safeguarded, because once we get into bad mental habits or something goes wrong in our mind it is difficult to put right.

8. "Disdaining the immoral" specifically refers to ignoring and deprecating those who have created any of the five heinous actions or any of the basic downfalls. This may be done out of anger or the wish to harm but also out of laziness or lethargy. Bodhisattvas are normally particularly concerned for the well-being of those who do wrong because they see that their misdeeds will bring them suffering.[26] There is no fault if by ignoring them we hope to correct their actions, protect others' minds or if getting involved is contrary to the code of conduct for the ordained. This transgression contravenes the ethical discipline of restraint from harmful action and is contrary to the practice of considering others more important than oneself.

XI.   **Not training for the sake of others' faith;**
        Doing too little for the good of living beings;

With compassion there is no non-virtue;
Readily accepting a wrong livelihood.

9. "Not training for the sake of others' faith": This transgression conflicts with the ethical discipline of creating virtue. A Bodhisattva should, except under circumstances that demand otherwise, practice restraint from actions contrary to the individual liberation vow of a monk or nun and proscribed in the Hearer Vehicle.[27] Such restraint is important in order to avoid destroying others' faith. It involves not taking alcohol or eating at the wrong time, not digging the earth, felling trees or touching fire. Negligence regarding these precepts may be due to lack of faith, a dislike for them, arrogance thinking a Bodhisattva does not need to observe them or may be due to other disturbing emotions. Such carelessness may also be due to laziness or lethargy.

Those who hold the individual liberation vow transgress it by not refraining from these actions. Since a Bodhisattva is concerned with protecting others' minds, careful and disciplined conduct is vital. Although these restrictions apply particularly to ordained Bodhisattvas, there is much in this respect that a lay Bodhisattva also needs to observe.

The protection of living beings depends to a large extent on the protection of their habitat. This is why the Buddha stressed the need to refrain from wantonly destroying the environment. Nowadays our concern about the environment focuses primarily on the harm we humans experience as a result of its pollution and exploitation. Though sometimes anger or hatred are responsible for the destruction we are witnessing, the main cause is our greed. We despoil our birthright for artificial wealth. By avoiding this kind of conduct we train ourselves in a way that conforms to the strong emphasis on non-attachment in the teachings of the Lesser Vehicle.

10. To avoid "doing too little for others' well-being" we must train in a way exclusive to the Great Vehicle. This transgression conflicts with the ethical discipline of working for

others. The Hearer Vehicle is concerned with personal liberation for which it is vital to combat attachment and craving by having few desires, few possessions and by adopting the four features characteristic of the exalted: simple food, clothing and shelter as well as a strong liking for meditation and for overcoming the faults and limitations which need to be discarded.[28] However, it is a mistake for Bodhisattvas to restrict themselves in this way as it may hamper their work for others. While they should, of course, curtail personal needs and desires, they are permitted to be acquisitive for the benefit of others.

At present we are insatiable regarding our own desires but easily satisfied when it comes to the fulfillment of others' needs. A Bodhisattva behaves in the opposite way. According to the Hearer Vehicle an ordained person should only accept limited alms. A Bodhisattva, however, accepts whatever is given and distributes the surplus to others. The Hearer Vehicle prescribes that certain robes in excess of the basic ones may be kept for only ten days, others for thirty days, and that they must be blessed and given away within the designated time. Preoccupation with such things is inappropriate for Bodhisattvas because it can act as a distraction from their work for others.

11. "With compassion there is no non-virtue": Although Asanga's *Bodhisattva Stages* and Chandragomin's *Twenty Verses* do not explicitly state that a Bodhisattva must be prepared to perform negative actions, commentaries, including Je Tsongkhapa's, mention that under certain circumstances it is a fault for a Bodhisattva not to perform normally negative actions out of compassion for others. The negative actions are the seven harmful actions of body and speech which are classed as natural non-virtue[29] and are never permitted according to the individual liberation vow. Lay Bodhisattvas must perform any of these seven if the circumstances demand it. Ordained Bodhisattvas may under no circumstances engage in sexual intercourse but must perform any of the

other six actions when necessary. To do so is not only not negative but creates much merit and will increase others' faith in the Bodhisattva.

Why may an ordained Bodhisattva never engage in sexual misconduct but may kill, steal or lie, since these are surely all defeats of the individual liberation vow? A defeat of the individual liberation vow is created the moment orgasm is experienced as a result of sexual intercourse, while in the case of the other activities, various factors must be present for the action to constitute a defeat. When a Bodhisattva who holds the individual liberation vow undertakes any of the other actions, these decisive factors must not be present and the action must never constitute an actual defeat. For example, Bodhisattvas may never steal for their own benefit but may steal for the benefit of others. If an ordained Bodhisattva is in a position where sexual intercourse for another's benefit is unavoidable, the Bodhisattva must first give back the individual liberation vow and thereby become a lay person.

These guidelines apply to ordinary Bodhisattvas—those on the paths of accumulation and preparation—who have the altruistic intention, hold the vow and are working for others through intensive practice of the six perfections. These Bodhisattvas have so much familiarity with their practice, gained throughout many previous aeons, that they are able to maintain a completely pure and virtuous state of mind from the preparation right through to the conclusion of any so-called negative action. Bodhisattvas may only perform such actions when they will be of great benefit to others, when no alternative means are available and no other person could perform the action. Strict criteria always apply and holding the Bodhisattva vow is never an excuse for indiscriminate conduct. The higher vows do not purify any transgressions of the individual liberation vow nor is the tantric vow an excuse for unethical behavior which pollutes the Buddha's teaching.

In a situation where someone is prepared to kill Bodhisattvas or other practitioners with high realizations for petty material gain, a Bodhisattva might recognize that as a result the criminal will have to take rebirth in the hells again and again. Without any self-concern and with true compassion the Bodhisattva kills the person who is about to commit murder. Not the slightest trace of any disturbing emotions but only a virtuous or neutral state of mind is present during the action. Under such circumstances nothing but merit can ensue.

A Bodhisattva's act of stealing or taking what has not been given may involve three main types of objects. The first consists of taking away power and authority from those who misuse them to harm living beings. I think it is excellent that the democratic process enables people of this kind to be removed constitutionally without violence. The second situation involves seizing things that belong to the spiritual community or to a stupa and which have been misappropriated by a thief, and returning them to their rightful owners or distributing them to the poor. The third situation is one in which the Bodhisattva takes over gardens, temples and other communal facilities which are being misused, used for private purposes or have been neglected and allowed to fall into disrepair in order to restore them and give others access to them. No self-interest should be involved.

A lay Bodhisattva may engage in sexual misconduct if the other person involved might otherwise bear strong resentment, act destructively or die, for instance by suicide. The Bodhisattva is motivated by the understanding that resentment will only lead to negative actions and by the compassionate wish to help the other person to lead a more constructive life.

Bodhisattvas may not lie for their own purposes but only to save another's life, to prevent them from being mutilated or to protect them from any other danger. No disturbing emotions should be involved and the motivation should be entirely altruistic.

Divisive speech is permitted when someone is under the influence of a bad spiritual friend or mentor who is encouraging them to do wrong. Seeing that the relationship will bring disaster in this and future lives, the Bodhisattva out of compassion speaks divisive words to bring about an estrangement.

Harsh words may be used to dissuade someone from following a wrong path but these should be spoken without anger. Not everything can be accomplished in a gentle manner. In traditional societies parents and teachers may sternly correct children in their care. Though the children don't like it at the time because it prevents them doing what they want, it does not lead to resentment. In the long run permissiveness may not really be kind.

Gossip and so forth is permitted to attract and please those who like music, dancing and light talk. The Bodhisattva should be skilled in these pastimes and motivated by the compassionate wish to exercise a positive influence over the person attracted so as to steer them away from wrong-doing. This may keep a friend from growing distant and bring someone distant close.

12. "Readily accepting a wrong livelihood" refers to accepting what is acquired through hypocrisy, flattery, hinting, extortion or giving little in the hope of receiving much without considering this a fault.[30] Disturbing emotions are always present in such cases. If we realize it is wrong to gain a livelihood in this way, try hard to stop but are still unable to avoid it, no transgression is created because it doesn't constitute ready acceptance of things gained by these means.

For ordained people scrupulous avoidance of the wrong ways of gaining a livelihood is essential and lay people should endeavor to earn a living in a decent, honest and positive way. Selling alcohol, poison, weapons, animals, dyes and glues, felling trees without care and pressing oil without examining the substance to be pressed for the presence of living beings are also considered faulty ways of earning a living according to the traditional texts. A Bodhisattva should not accept what has been acquired through destructive activities, for by doing so he or she has deviated from a pure livelihood.

XII.   Getting very excited through distraction;
      Thinking to travel only in cyclic existence;
      Failing to prevent defamation;
      Not correcting even [those] with disturbing emotions.

13. "Getting very excited through distraction" refers to agitation stemming from desire which distracts the mind and makes it unpeaceful and unruly. This causes excited physical and verbal activity: horseplay, joking, fooling around and encouraging others to do the same. When this is done out of carelessness without the presence of desire, it is a transgression without disturbing emotions. The Bodhisattva has deviated from pure conduct.

14. "Thinking to travel only in cyclic existence": In sutra there are statements that Bodhisattvas love samsara but do not like nirvana nearly as much. It is a misinterpretation to think that Bodhisattvas need not take an interest in liberation nor fear the disturbing emotions and make every effort to rid themselves of them, but that they must remain in cyclic existence for countless aeons to gain complete enlightenment. To hold such a belief and express it is the result of confusion and misunderstanding and constitutes this transgression.

Do Bodhisattvas like nirvana or not? They like it a hundred thousand times more than Hearers and Solitary Realizers. Their dislike for the disturbing emotions is so strong that they make an even greater effort to rid themselves of them because they have vowed to attain enlightenment for all living beings. Though unlike Foe Destroyers they have not yet freed themselves entirely of the disturbing emotions, they regard them as enemies and learn to encounter the objects of the senses without allowing these emotions to arise. The meaning of such sutra passages is that they must not turn towards nirvana and forget about taking rebirth again and again for the sake of all living beings.

15. "Failing to prevent defamation": A Bodhisattva may rightly or wrongly be accused of saying what is meaningless or unreliable. If there is some basis for the accusation and the Bodhisattva does not take steps to improve his or her communication skills, the faulty action is created with disturbing emotions. If the accusation is unfounded, but the Bodhisattva does nothing to counter it, the faulty action is created without disturbing emotions. Bodhisattvas must protect their reputation and avoid defamation because unless they are seen as trustworthy, their interaction with and work for others will be hampered. There is no fault in not taking action if the defamer is set on ruining the Bodhisattva's reputation and would not take any notice of what the Bodhisattva might say or if the defamer is extremely angry and the situation might simply be aggravated. When Bodhisattvas are disparaged for doing something which it is quite proper for them to do, such as taking ordination vows, practicing virtue or begging for alms, there is no fault in not doing anything to ward off the defamation.

16. "Not correcting even [those] with disturbing emotions": If a Bodhisattva sees the physical or verbal misconduct of another person and realizes that stern speech and demeanor could correct this but fails to employ such an approach for fear of being disliked and losing popularity, the faulty action is created with disturbing emotions. If it will make the other person very unhappy and there is little benefit to be gained by speaking or acting harshly, there is no fault in not doing so. The previous nine transgressions are contrary to the practice of the perfection of ethical discipline.

XIII.   Abuse in return for abuse, and so forth;
Ignoring those who are angry;

Disregarding another's excuses;
Following thoughts of anger.

The next four transgressions are contrary to the practice of the perfection of patience. A Bodhisattva thinks often of the faults of anger and the great benefits of patience. This helps to sustain the one and curtail the other.

17. "Abuse in return for abuse, and so forth": If Bodhisattvas react to abuse, anger, physical violence and to the pointing out of their hidden faults by responding in kind, they create this faulty action. By doing so they deviate from the practice of virtue, which involves not responding to provocation in such a way, and they fail to maintain the conditions which further patience. "Striking them in anger," which is similar and is part of the third basic downfall, concerns initiating physical aggression and not the reaction to it.

18. "Ignoring those who are angry": The Bodhisattva may have angered someone by a wrong action or the other person may be angry because he or she mistakenly suspects the Bodhisattva of wrong-doing. If out of anger, envy or pride the Bodhisattva does nothing to dispel the other's anger, the faulty action is created with disturbing emotions. If the Bodhisattva has done nothing wrong and doesn't care what the other person thinks, the fault is created without disturbing emotions. Anger should not be allowed to continue. In either situation it is vital to do what is necessary to restore a good relationship. If the Bodhisattva thinks that by doing nothing, the other person will be helped in the long run, there is no fault. If he or she suspects the anger is merely a means of extracting an apology or that an apology would be of no use because the other person will persist in holding a wrong view, there is no fault.

19. "Disregarding another's excuses": If someone who has acted wrongly tries to apologize and the Bodhisattva refuses to accept the apology out of anger, pride and so forth, the transgression is created with disturbing emotions. If the Bodhisattva feels embarrassed by or is too lazy to deal with

the apology, it is created without disturbing emotions. In the case of "not heeding the confession of others," which is similar and forms part of the third basic downfall, anger that has been harbored in the form of strong resentment is always present. No fault is created by not accepting the apology if the other person can be helped by this or if the apology is insincere.

20. "Following thoughts of anger": The transgression is created if we follow angry thoughts, see nothing wrong with such thoughts and make no effort to stop them by applying counteractions. If we realize angry thoughts are counterproductive, and sincerely try to stop them but fail, the transgression is not created. This and the previous transgression sustain the continuity of anger.

I remember hearing that the monk in charge of discipline at my local monastery in eastern Tibet was told by his teacher to look up in the air and not to watch the monks while they were assembling and taking their seats. He was not to look at them until they had settled down. Then he would see quite a lot of them sitting properly and wouldn't feel annoyed. In case he needed to discipline anyone, he should first go outside, calm down and then use the rod or take whatever action was necessary. Many monks in charge of discipline used to make a point of always taking some time to calm their irritation before saying anything.

XIV.   Gathering followers out of desire for reward and respect;
Not getting rid of laziness and so forth;
Indulging in gossip with passion;
Not seeking the object of meditative stabilization.

The next three transgressions are contrary to the practice of the perfection of enthusiastic effort. Enthusiastic effort is the delight in virtue.

21. "Gathering followers out of desire for reward and respect": This transgression is created if one gathers students out of a craving for material gain or for gestures of respect,

such as being assisted when taking a bath, having one's seat prepared or being spared any kind of work. A Bodhisattva should attract students but certainly not to exploit them.

22. "Not getting rid of laziness and so forth": The transgression is created through indulging in the pleasure that comes from different forms of indolence, such as lounging around, lolling this way and that and sleeping excessively, not only during the night but during the day as well. The first and last parts of the night should ideally be devoted to practice and only the middle of the night to sleep. There is no fault if one is sick, exhausted from traveling or trying hard to stop these habits.

23. The transgression of "indulging in gossip with passion" is created with disturbing emotions if one avidly listens to or tells stories about those in positions of power, about robberies, amazing events or erotic episodes for hours and hours during the day or late into the night. If one tells or listens to these stories without much fascination or interest but just gets caught and finds it impossible to excuse oneself, the transgression is created without disturbing emotions. If one listens for a reasonable time out of courtesy, there is no fault, nor if one asks someone to tell an amazing or funny story or is requested to do so for relaxation and amusement. A person who can do this is an asset at a Tibetan party or picnic, otherwise everyone soon turns to playing cards or dice.

The following three transgressions are contrary to the perfection of concentration and interfere with preparation for its practice, the practice itself and the necessary conclusion.

24. "Not seeking the object of meditative stabilization": It is a Bodhisattva's responsibility to develop concentration. Spiritual teachers should be well versed in the three kinds of training—in ethical discipline, concentration and wisdom—and rich in knowledge of the three categories of scriptures concerning the code of ethical discipline for the ordained, sutra and higher knowledge. They should also be

motivated by a compassionate wish to free students from suffering and not by desire for material gain.

The Buddha himself said mantra recitation and other practices of virtue will lack power and efficacy without concentration, the mind's ability to remain fixed on a positive focal object. Mindfulness is the mental activity which enables this because it prevents loss of the focal object. Mental alertness contributes by checking that the concentration is proceeding as intended.

If one intends to concentrate on a focal object, but out of harmful intent, anger, pride or the like fails to listen to instructions on how to do so, the transgression is created with disturbing emotions. If one's failure to listen stems from indolence or laziness, which is a lack of interest in virtue, it is created without disturbing emotions. This transgression acts as an obstacle to starting the practice of concentration. There is no fault if the Bodhisattva is incapable of listening, suspects misleading instructions will be given or already has complete knowledge of what is involved in the practice.

XV.   **Not eliminating the hindrances to concentration;**
       Appreciating the taste of concentration;
       Giving up the Hearer Vehicle;
       Effort in that, despite having one's own method.

25. "Not eliminating the hindrances to concentration": There are five obstacles to concentration which also act as obstacles to the three kinds of training. They are mentioned in many texts and Nagarjuna calls them the robbers who steal our wealth of virtue. They are (1) excitement and regret, (2) harmful thoughts, (3) sleep and foggy-mindedness, (4) desire for sense objects and (5) doubt. If these occur and we make no effort to eliminate them, the transgression is created with disturbing emotions. If we try hard but do not succeed, there is no fault.

Excitement is an aspect of desire. Agitation which is caused by anger is not termed "excitement" but is identified as distraction, one of the twenty secondary disturbing emotions.

Mental wandering caused by virtuous thoughts is also a type of distraction but is not classed as a disturbing emotion. In the practice of concentration every kind of distraction is undesirable and must be dealt with right away. More distraction is caused by underlying desire than by anger.

Like excitement, regret focuses on one's own or others' actions. It is a heavy feeling caused by thoughts of friends and loved ones, of places such as one's country, of past pleasures and things one has enjoyed, as well as by thinking about what one has done or so far failed to do and by the thought that one will not die. Regret is a great distraction. We Tibetans often remember our country: how unpolluted the air and water were; how on a summer's day, if you sat on a little knoll, the refreshing fragrance of grass, flowers and medicinal plants came wafting on the breeze—a natural spa. No need for anything artificial. Such nostalgic thoughts produce regret and are a source of distraction in meditation.

Harmful thoughts are those of wanting to hurt others, wishing them misfortune and so forth. Such thoughts arise when we regard others as disagreeable. Then thinking about their behavior and appearance we can become so incensed that if they were in our presence, we would strike them.

Unconsciously we arouse strong desire or anger by thinking over and over again about various aspects of the object, which stimulates either of these emotions. The same procedure can consciously be employed to arouse positive emotions like compassion, love, the altruistic intention, an understanding of impermanence and so forth. Although analytical meditation of this kind has a most powerful transformative effect, which is actually the true aim of meditation, many beginners have a resistance to it and prefer placement meditation in the form of single-pointed concentration on a focal object. The ideal procedure is to alternate analytical and placement meditation by, for instance, using analytical meditation to arouse a specific positive emotion and then to sustain it for some time through placement meditation which focuses on that feeling.

Sleep is an aspect of confusion and a withdrawal of awareness from objects, particularly those that act as sense stimuli. We spend so much time asleep that if our sleep is negative or neutral, we waste half our life, so we should take care to make the most of sleep. Although only practitioners with developed control of the mind can take advantage of the clear light, a subtle state of awareness that occurs during deep sleep, we can at least make our sleep positive by thinking good thoughts as we fall asleep. Controlling the mind while we are awake is something we can reasonably aim to do, but most of us have little interest in this and are fascinated by sleep and dream yoga. Our ears prick up the moment these are mentioned.

Foggy-mindedness, like sleep, is an aspect of confusion and a heaviness, lethargy and unserviceability of the body and mind. It makes the mind unclear and one feels discouraged or depressed. Both sleep and foggy-mindedness are induced by a sense of mental darkness or dullness. They easily give rise to slackness during the practice of concentration and prevent clarity.

Desire for sense objects arises when we exaggerate the attractiveness of something through an incorrect mental approach and become preoccupied with our craving for it.

Doubt focuses on past, present or future phenomena. Employing an incorrect mental approach when we engage with them gives rise to doubt. Engaging with them correctly, by seeing them as they are, dispels doubt. In the context of the teachings doubt may focus on issues such as the existence of past and future lives, the connection between actions and their effects, the four noble truths, the qualities of the Three Jewels and so forth.

To counteract desire for sense objects we must deal with our exaggeration of their attractiveness by thinking about their unattractive aspects. Harmful thoughts are counteracted by cultivating love and compassion. Once we truly cannot bear to watch others suffer nor even to see them do what will later bring them suffering, how could we wish to harm them?

Sleep and foggy-mindedness are counteracted by making the mind brighter and more lively. This can be done by thinking about the richness of our human life, the inspiring qualities of the Three Jewels, the great benefits of practicing generosity, ethics or patience and so forth. Excitement and regret are counteracted by effort to keep the mind single-pointed on its focal object according to the methods described for the development of calm abiding. Doubt is counteracted by understanding the existence of that which actually exists and the non-existence of things that do not exist. When we think something which doesn't exist exists, we are fabricating and superimposing. When we take something that exists to be non-existent, we underestimate its status.

Conscientiousness in not letting disturbing emotions get the upper hand is an essential aspect of practice. The Bodhisattva must stop these emotions from arising and must curtail their duration when they do occur. This demands constant mindfulness and vigilance. The hindrances to concentration are presented from an entirely practical point of view and learning about them should be for the purpose of eliminating them. First they are identified and defined. Since the next step is to understand what causes them, the process by which they arise is then discussed. In order to stop them we must know their antidotes and how to apply them effectively.

If the hindrances to concentration affected only those trying to achieve meditative stabilization, everything would be solved by avoiding the practice of concentration. But they affect us all, whether we are Buddhists or non-Buddhists, whether we try to meditate or not, and removing them is to our advantage even in the context of daily life. By watching the mind we can begin to rid ourselves of what harms and causes us misery. When those factors grow weaker our real happiness begins. This is the mark of all authentic spiritual practice. If we misuse our spiritual tradition to foster hostility and hatred, we destroy it from within and turn a god into a devil.

We should look to great practitioners of the past as role-models. One such was Milarepa,[31] who went to the mountains to engage in intensive practice. He lived in caves and ate the plants that grew nearby. This shows us the importance of having few desires and cultivating contentment. In all spiritual traditions there have been great practitioners who chose to live a simple life. The greed of constantly wanting this and that, and lack of contentment with what we have, take up much of our time and energy and are a serious distraction. We may have few possessions but if we are content, we will feel rich. No matter how rich we are, if we aren't satisfied, we always feel poor.

26. "Appreciating the taste of concentration": This transgression can occur when we have developed concentration. We may be attached to the joy it brings or proud of what we have achieved and become fixated on the experience of concentration and the feelings it induces. If we see the drawbacks of this and try to stop it but fail, there is no fault.

Craving for the peace and well-being induced by concentration, pride in it, ignorance and wrong views associated with it make the concentration unwholesome and deluded. They prevent its continuity and enhancement.

The next transgressions are contrary to the practice of the perfection of wisdom. Some focus on the teachings of the Lesser Vehicle and non-Buddhist teachings, while others focus on the teachings of the Great Vehicle.

27. "Giving up the Hearer Vehicle": This transgression is created if we think or say that it is unnecessary to listen to teachings of the Lesser Vehicle, to remember the words and meaning of those teachings or to try and put them into practice. Since in order to help others Bodhisattvas need to be conversant even with non-Buddhist teachings, they should clearly not ignore the teachings of the Lesser Vehicle, which

were given by the Buddha. No fault is created by advising someone who is inclined towards the Great Vehicle but is spending excessive time on practices associated with the Lesser Vehicle not to do so, in order to prevent them from turning away from the Great Vehicle.

28. "Effort in that, despite having one's own method": We have access to the Mahayana scriptures which clearly describe what we should practice. The transgression is created when, instead of putting the main emphasis on these, we devote too much time and energy to practices associated with the Lesser Vehicle. We should concentrate mainly on Mahayana practices but at the same time put into practice the teachings of the Lesser Vehicle.

XVI. Without effort except for non-Buddhist treatises;
      Making effort and also liking them;
      Rejecting the Great Vehicle;
      Praising oneself or disparaging others.

29. "Without effort except for non-Buddhist treatises": The Buddha's teaching in general is worthy of our attention and effort. The transgression is created if we favor non-Buddhist teachings and devote much effort to studying them. We should not pursue novelty. It is important to open the four windows and let the breeze blow in but at the same time we must make sure that we aren't blown away. We are wise if we can accept good advice wherever it may be found and stupid if we remain in our birthplace or cling to old ideas when they don't bring us any benefit.

On the other hand, when climbing a tree, only a fool will let go of one branch before firmly catching hold of the next. Similarly, it is unwise to give up our own spiritual tradition or philosophical position before we feel comfortable in another. There is no fault in putting effort into studying non-Buddhist teachings if we are also making a thorough study of the Buddha's teachings, have a stable mind and are intelligent.

30. "Making effort and also liking them": The transgression is created if we put effort into the study of non-Buddhist teachings and throughout take particular delight in what we are doing. Such pleasure may influence us to turn away from the Mahayana teachings. We should undertake the study of non-Buddhist teachings simply to be well-informed and when there is a specific positive purpose for doing so.

The Mahayana teachings contain all that is needed to attain enlightenment. Other spiritual traditions may or may not speak about personal enlightenment. If they do, the enlightenment to which they refer and the methods leading to it may or may not be the same as those which the teachings of the Great Vehicle describe. If they are the same, there is no good reason for abandoning the methods we already have and with which we are familiar. Although this implies that there is no better way than that laid out by the Mahayana teachings, it does not mean that all other teachings are inferior.

31. "Rejecting the Great Vehicle": The transgression consists of disparaging the profound or extensive teachings of the Great Vehicle. What leads to this? The teachings of the Great Vehicle, for instance those contained in the Perfection of Wisdom Sutras, speak of very profound matters beyond the understanding even of Hearers and Solitary Realizers, let alone ordinary people. They also mention the extraordinary powers of Bodhisattvas and enlightened beings. Those who are unable to understand these things may reject them.

By misunderstanding the statements in the Perfection of Wisdom Sutras that nothing has inherent existence to mean that nothing exists, the subject-matter of these sutras may be rejected on the grounds that it is inferior and unable to produce real wisdom. The words used to express the subject-matter may be rejected as inferior and incapable of giving rise to merit because they are regarded as propagating nihilism or exaggerating the qualities possessed by Buddhas and Bodhisattvas. Their author may be rejected as inferior by thinking that the Perfection of Wisdom sutras are not the Buddha's words. Such conclusions can result from an incorrect mental approach or from others' influence. The transgression may involve rejecting either the profound or extensive aspects of the Great Vehicle and differs from the basic downfall, "rejecting the Great Vehicle," which entails rejecting the whole of the Great Vehicle.

If we feel a lack of belief or conviction regarding certain aspects of the teachings, rather than dismissing them it is wise to think that we are perhaps at present not yet capable of a proper understanding. There are passages that seem to be specifically relevant to social conditions prevailing at the Buddha's time. Others may seem hostile to women but were, in fact, directed at male practitioners to counter their lust. Both men and women have the same capacity to attain enlightenment and both men and women need to develop the wish to get out of cyclic existence, the altruistic intention and the correct understanding of reality. From the point of view of tantra, both men and women must practice the stages of generation and completion.

This being so, people sometimes wonder why the Buddha hesitated before ordaining women. His purpose in conferring ordination was to benefit others and perhaps he thought that due to the prevailing social conditions women would find it difficult to keep the vow of an ordained person.

Although in this aeon there have been only male Buddhas[32] who have manifested a supreme emanation body and acted as world teachers, there may have been female ones before. Who is to say there will be none in future? When being born into a royal or Brahmin family has been esteemed, Buddhas have taken such a birth. If women have higher status than men in a particular society, an enlightened being might well appear in a female supreme emanation body. The major and minor marks which are described as adorning such a body are those displayed by the Buddha Shakyamuni, features considered beautiful at that time, but they could conceivably be different. They are called "good signs."[33]

32. "Praising oneself or disparaging others": This transgression is created if we do either of these out of pride or animosity. In the case of the first basic downfall the motivation is craving reward or respect for oneself. According to Mahayana teaching, desire is normally considered less serious than anger, yet we find that praising oneself or belittling others out of desire for reward and respect is a basic downfall, while doing it out of anger is a minor transgression. I do not know the reason for this.

XVII.   **Not to go for the teachings;**
        Deprecating them and relying upon the letter;
        Not being a friend in need;
        Refusing to serve the sick.

33. "Not to go for the teachings": The transgression is created with disturbing emotions by not attending teachings or talks associated with the Buddha's teachings, for instance those on the history of Buddhism, out of pride, hostility, a wish to hurt and so forth. The transgression may also be created out of laziness. This indicates the importance of making the effort to broaden our perspective by extensive exposure to many different aspects of Buddhism. There is no fault if we were not aware that the event was taking place, are sick, suspect that the information or teachings will be incorrect, have heard them many times, are conversant with and have understood them well or if we lack the intelligence to grasp what is being taught. There is also no fault if we are studying other topics, learning texts by heart, or are cultivating the altruistic intention or meditative stabilization. If the teachings are good, the teacher is reputable and we feel attracted but our own spiritual teacher would prefer that we did not attend, no error is created by not doing so.

34. "Deprecating them and relying upon the letter": The transgression is created with disturbing emotions if we intentionally disparage the person who is teaching, do not look

upon him or her as an enlightened being and as our spiritual teacher nor show appropriate physical or verbal respect. Our attention may be focused critically on the words being used to communicate the teaching and not on the intended meaning. The great texts advise us to concentrate on the meaning and not to get caught up with the words. People are often fascinated by a good speaker and fail to consider whether what has been said is actually true.

35. "Not being a friend in need": The first activity mentioned under the ethical discipline of working for others is to provide friendship and support. This has eight aspects: the first is to think about how to make others, who have actual or potential problems, materially secure. The second is to take active responsibility for protecting and increasing their resources. The third is to assist those in need of help who are coming or going and who have no one else to help them. The fourth is to teach a stranger who does not speak the local language. The fifth is to help with work such as agriculture or business provided it does not involve us in faulty activities. The sixth is to insure that others' property is not lost, for instance to thieves or robbers. The seventh is to facilitate the resolution of conflicts and to help the parties involved to overcome their hostility and resentment. Any resolution will be short-lived unless the underlying resentment is dispelled. The mediation may be between countries or persons. The eighth is to encourage those whose situation is good to increase their merit by making offerings on auspicious days.

The transgression of not being a friend in need is created with disturbing emotions if we are in a position to do these things but don't out of hostility, pride or for other similar reasons. It is created without disturbing emotions if we neglect to offer our help because of laziness. There is no fault if we are sick, have already promised to help someone else, have asked someone else to help instead, are involved in some other important activity or are incapable of helping in the way that is needed.

36. "Refusing to serve the sick": The transgression is a particular instance contravening the practice of helping those who are suffering. If the sick person is unable to manage alone and there is no one else to help, we should provide assistance. The transgression is created with disturbing emotions if we fail to do so out of pride, hostility and so forth. It may also be created out of laziness. We are often ready to offer assistance when we know that others are also involved but we feel afraid to take the full responsibility of caring for a sick person and so stay away if no one else is helping. There is no fault if we are doing other important work for the greater good. From this it is evident that the Mahayana teachings contain clear instructions regarding the importance of caring for the sick.

XVIII. Not removing suffering;
     Not teaching the careless what is proper;
     Not repaying a good deed[34];
     Not assuaging others' grief.

37. "Not removing suffering": We should assist the blind, deaf, disabled and those who are simply doddery as well as those who are displaced, dispossessed, disparaged or reviled. We should help those who are crippled in and out of conveyances, assist those who are suffering from the five hindrances to concentration and also those who are full of superstition, preconceptions and busy thoughts. The transgression consists of not helping when there is an opportunity to do so. It may be created with or without disturbing emotions. A Bodhisattva must be wise and know how best to assist others. We shouldn't think that we are excused from helping simply because we are not yet Bodhisattvas!

In modern times there are all kinds of public and private organizations to help disabled people and facilities for counseling those in need of assistance. When the Buddha laid down these guidelines for Bodhisattvas such facilities did not exist. A Bodhisattva willingly accepts responsibility and is ready to interfere in a positive way. Who is to say that guide dogs for the blind or dolphins that rescue people at sea are not in fact Bodhisattvas?

Once in Pempo[35] in Central Tibet there was a rich woman who owned a lot of property but had no children. She went to one of the Kadampa masters and told him that she felt miserable because she was childless and could he please help her to have a child. He said to her, "You're suffering now because you have no child, but you would suffer much more if you had one. Imagine if all the people in Pempo were your children. You'd be crying from morning till night because one of them would always be dying." Bodhisattvas have greater affection for all living beings than a mother's affection for her children, but because of the depth of their insight and wisdom they are not overwhelmed by grief when they see others suffer.

38. "Not teaching the careless what is proper": The transgression is created if we realize that someone is engaged in a wrong and harmful course of action and have the power to correct this but neglect to do so because of our negative emotions or laziness. There is no fault if we don't have sufficient knowledge or ability to help, if the person can help him or herself, if someone else is already helping and giving advice, if the person doesn't like one, if one's attempt to help may simply make matters worse or if more will be achieved by doing nothing. Although all this appears quite straightforward, many problems we encounter are the result of not being able to decide on the appropriate form of behavior towards others.

39. "Not repaying a good deed": The transgression is created if we do not know how to, do not remember to or do not wish to repay kindness shown to us. This may be because of disturbing emotions or laziness. There is no fault if we want to repay the good deed but do not find an opportunity.

40. "Not assuaging others' grief": The transgression is created if we do nothing to comfort those who are grieving over the loss of a parent, a beloved partner or child, a trusted and reliable friend or companion, a precious spiritual teacher,

the loss of personal property or wealth or their home and country. The transgression may be created because of disturbing emotions or laziness.

XIX.   **Not giving to those who want wealth;**
Not working for the welfare of followers;
Not conforming to others' ideas;
Not speaking in praise of good qualities.

41. "Not giving to those who want wealth": The transgression is created if, out of disturbing emotions or laziness, we do not give food, clothing or money to those who ask for them. There is no fault if we do not possess what has been demanded or think the person may be induced to stand on his or her own feet by refusing the request.

42. "Not working for the welfare of followers": The transgression is created out of disturbing emotions or laziness if we do not look after the spiritual or material welfare of followers we may have acquired. The emphasis here is on the Bodhisattva's responsibility not to exploit but to benefit followers. They should be given teaching again and again and provided with honestly acquired food, clothing and whatever is needed. We have only to look at the example of politicians who promise much to their followers, but once elected fail to deliver. There is no fault if we are sick, have asked someone else to help who is capable of doing so, think that followers can be better helped by not doing anything or if by not teaching or giving them material aid we can protect them from punishment.

43. "Not conforming to others' ideas": We must endeavor to relate to others in a manner which conforms to their way of thinking and should try our best to do what they want. Not doing so because of disturbing emotions or laziness creates the transgression. But should one always do what they want? There is no fault if an action would harm them, or harm us in any way, since we need our strength to work for other living beings. There is also no fault if a particular

action would help and satisfy the other person but upset many others. Most of the guidelines regarding the ethical discipline of working for others concern how to conduct relationships with them.

44. "Not speaking in praise of good qualities": The transgression may be created because of disturbing emotions or laziness. We should be generous with praise for those with good qualities such as sincere generosity, knowledge of the teachings, good ethical conduct, a stable mind and so forth. When others receive well-deserved praise, we should express our agreement. There is no fault if we are unable to express praise, no opportunity to do so arises or if the person to be praised would find it embarrassing.

XX.   Not punishing to fit the circumstances;
        Not using miraculous feats to threaten and so forth.
        There is no fault if one has compassion,
        Is loving and has a virtuous mind.

45. "Not punishing to fit the circumstances": We may create the transgression with or without disturbing emotions by not taking the opportunity to administer the correct kind of punishment to a wrongdoer as a deterrent. It may be necessary to demote, punish or expel the person. We must be skilled enough to decide whether the circumstances demand a lenient or severe punishment, for example an expulsion of limited duration or complete expulsion. There is no fault if we are waiting for the right opportunity, if the person is obstinate and will be unaffected by punishment, if inflicting a punishment will make things worse, or if we think that out of a sense of shame or decency the person concerned will in due course spontaneously correct the behavior in question.

46. "Not using miraculous feats to threaten and so forth": The transgression is created if we do not use miraculous powers we possess to threaten wrongdoers or to give them a good fright by, for instance, manifesting a hell realm; if we do not use our powers to inspire faith, belief, conviction and

aspiration or to prevent the negative actions of those who are taking advantage of offerings and respect by pretending still to hold the vows of a monk or nun. Failure to use these powers may be motivated by disturbing emotions or simply by laziness.

Chandragomin's text ends with the words, "There is no fault if one has compassion, is loving and has a virtuous mind." In the context of the forty-six minor transgressions we learn of many things the Bodhisattva should do. Not to do them creates the transgression. If the Bodhisattva is motivated by love, compassion, the wish to help and train others and is able to maintain a virtuous state of mind from the inception until the conclusion of a particular action, there is no fault in not doing what should be done and in doing what should not be done.

If we do not hold the vow, we cannot create any transgression of it. Nor do we create transgressions if we are seriously disturbed and not in a sane state of mind. Where certain transgressions are concerned, there is no fault if despite genuine efforts to correct our behavior and counter disturbing emotions, the behavior nevertheless recurs. There is no fault if the action is performed in dream.

A Bodhisattva will only be able to help others effectively if the help is based on the ethical discipline of refraining from harm. Although we are not Bodhisattvas, many of us hold the vow and have therefore promised to devote ourselves to helping others. We wouldn't think of undertaking certain kinds of professional work such as nursing, counseling or practicing as a psychotherapist without any training. These guidelines for a Bodhisattva's conduct are like a program of training and offer very practical advice for our relationships and work with others. They also provide direction regarding more subtle and invisible aspects of that work such as motivation, how to prevent exhaustion and how to conclude an action in the most positive way.

People often view the individual liberation vow, particularly becoming ordained as a monk or nun, with awe but do not hesitate to take the Bodhisattva vow. After studying Chandragomin's *Twenty Verses* we will have some idea of the vast commitment the Bodhisattva vow involves. Normally when people mention "commitments" in the context of the Buddha's teachings, they are referring to daily practices, such as the performance of deity yoga or the recitation of mantras, and they are anxious to find a way of being included in a special category which permits them to do the shortest form of the practice because of their workload, studies or other circumstances. If we wish to honor the promise we make when we take the Bodhisattva vow, complete dedication and wholehearted commitment are needed.

Text of the *Twenty Verses* in English and Tibetan

CHANDRAGOMIN'S *TWENTY VERSES ON THE BODHISATTVA VOW*, supplemented by the verses from Shantideva's *Compendium of Training*

Homage to youthful Manjushri!

I. Pay homage with reverence and offer what you can

    To the Buddhas and their children.

    This is the code of Bodhisattvas

    Existing everywhere, throughout time.

II. Take that treasury of all merit,

    With an excellent intention,

    From a spiritual teacher with ability

    Who observes the vow and is learned in it.

༄༅། །རྒྱ་གར་སྐད་དུ། བོ་དྷི་སཏྭ་སཾ་བ་ར་བིཾ་ཤ་ཀ །
བོད་སྐད་དུ། །བྱང་ཆུབ་སེམས་དཔའི་སྡོམ་པ་ཉི་ཤུ་པ།

འཇམ་དཔལ་གཞོན་ནུར་གྱུར་པ་ལ་ཕྱག་འཚལ་ལོ།

༡　སངས་རྒྱས་སྲས་དང་བཅས་པ་ལ།
　　གུས་པས་ཕྱག་འཚལ་ཏེ་ནུས་མཆོད།
　　ཕྱོགས་དུས་ཀུན་ན་བཞུགས་པ་ཡི།
　　བྱང་ཆུབ་སེམས་པ་རྣམས་ཀྱི་ཁྲིམས།

༢　བསོད་ནམས་ཀུན་གྱི་གཏེར་གྱུར་གང་།
　　དེ་ནི་བསམ་པ་དམ་པ་ཡིས།
　　བླ་མ་སྟོབ་པ་གནས་ཞིང་མཁས།
　　ནུས་དང་ལྡན་ལ་བླང་བར་བྱ།

III.   Then, because it is definite,

         Buddhas and their children

         With their virtuous hearts will always

         Consider you their beloved child.

IV.   For others and also for yourself,

         Do what is useful even if painful,

         And what is both useful and pleasurable,

         Not what gives pleasure but is of no use.

V.   Coming from strong disturbing emotions,

         They are what destroy the vow.

         All four of their transgressions

         Are considered to be like defeats.

VI.   With attachment to reward, respect and service,

         Praising oneself or disparaging others;

         Out of miserliness not giving teaching

         Or wealth to the suffering and unprotected.

VII.   Not heeding the confession of others;

         Striking them in anger;

༣ དེ་ཚེ་དེ་ལ་རེས་པའི་ཕྱིར།

གྲུལ་བ་སྲས་དང་བཅས་རྣམས་ཀྱིས།

དགེ་བའི་ཕྱོགས་ཀྱིས་རྟག་པར་ཡང་།

བུ་ཕྲུག་འདྲ་བར་དགོངས་པར་འགྱུར།

༤ གཞན་རྣམས་དང་ནི་བདག་ལ་ཡང་རུང་།

ཕྱུག་བསྲུང་ཡིན་ཡང་གང་ཕན་དང་།

ཕན་དང་བདེ་བ་རྣམས་བྱུ་སྟེ།

བདེ་ཡང་མི་ཕན་མི་བྱེད་དོ།

༥ ཉིན་མོངས་དྲག་ལས་བྱུང་བ་ཡིས།

སྐྱོམ་པ་ཞིག་པར་གང་གྱུར་པ།

དེ་ཡི་ཉེས་པ་བཞི་པོ་ནི།

ཕམ་པ་འདྲ་བ་དགོངས་པ་ཡིན།

༦ ཉིད་དང་བགྱུར་སྟེ་ཆགས་པ་ཡིས།

བདག་བསྟོད་གཞན་ལ་སྨོད་པ་དང་།

ཕྱུག་བསྲུལ་མགོན་མེད་འགྱུར་པ་ལ།

སེར་སྣས་ཆོས་ནོར་མི་སྟེར་དང་།

༧ གཞན་གྱི་བཤགས་ཀྱང་མི་ཉན་པར།

ཁྲོས་ནས་གཞན་ལ་འཚོག་པ་དང་།

Rejecting the Great Vehicle;

Giving a counterfeit of the excellent teachings.

VIII.   The vow should be taken again.

Confess moderate contamination to three,

And to one. The rest, with and without disturbing emotions,

Are similarly [confessed in] one's own mind.

The intermediate lines are supplemented from Shantideva's Compendium of Training:

Robbing what belongs to the Three Jewels

Is a downfall likened to a defeat.

Rejecting the excellent teachings

Is named as the second by the Subduer.

The third is to seize the robes,

Strike or put in prison,

Demote from ordination or deprive of life

Even a monk with faulty discipline.

Performing the five heinous actions,

Holding wrong views,

Also destroying villages and so forth

Were said to be basic downfalls by the Subduer.

ཐེག་པ་ཆེན་པོ་སློང་བྱེད་ཅིང་།།

དམ་ཚིག་འདར་སྲུང་སློན་པའོ།།

༦ སྟོམ་པ་སྐྱར་ཡང་བླང་བར་བྱ།།

ཟབ་པ་འབྱིང་ནི་གསུམ་ལ་བ་ཤགས།།

གཅིག་གི་མདུན་དུ་ལྷག་མ་རྣམས།།

ཉིན་མོངས་མི་མོངས་བདག་སེམས་བཞིན།།

ཿ ། བསྐབ་བཏུས་ལས།

དགོན་མཆོག་གསུམ་གྱི་དགོར་འཕོགས་པ།།

ཕས་ཕམ་པ་ཨེ་ལྱུང་བར་འདོད།།

དམ་པའི་ཆོས་ནི་སློང་བྱེད་པ།།

གཉིས་པར་ཐུབ་པས་གསུངས་པ་ཨིན།།

ཚུལ་ཁྲིམས་འཆལ་བའི་དགེ་སློང་ལའང་།།

དར་སྐྱིག་འཕོགས་པ་བརྗེགས་པ་དང་།།

བཙོན་རར་འཇུག་པར་བྱེད་པ་དང་།།

རབ་ཏུ་བྱུང་ལས་འབེབས་པ་དང་།།

སྲོག་དང་འབྲལ་བྱེད་གསུམ་པ་ཨིན།།

མཚམས་མེད་ལྔ་པོ་བྱེད་པ་དང་།།

ལོག་པར་ལྟ་བ་འཛིན་པ་དང་།།

གྲོང་ལ་སོགས་པ་འཇིག་པ་ལའང་།།

རྒྱ་བའི་ལྱང་བར་ཐུབ་པས་གསུངས།།

Speaking about emptiness to a living being

Whose mind has not been prepared;

Making those engaged in [attaining] Buddhahood

Turn away from complete enlightenment;

After they have given up individual liberation,

Involving them in the Great Vehicle.

Saying and convincing them that the Learners' Vehicle

Cannot eliminate attachment and so forth;

Also making them enter [the Great Vehicle].

Speaking about one's own good qualities

And disparaging others for reward, respect

And for the sake of verses.

Saying what is false [such as]

"I can tolerate the profound."

Having practitioners of virtue fined,

And accepting what was given

And donated to the Three Jewels.

Making them give up calm abiding

And giving to those who perform recitation

The resources of practitioners of concentration—

These are the basic downfalls

བློ་སྒྲུང་མ་བྱས་སེམས་ཅན་ལ།
སྤྱོང་བ་ཉིད་ནི་བརྗོད་པ་དང་།
སངས་རྒྱས་ཉིད་ལ་བཞུགས་པ་རྣམས།
རྟོགས་པའི་བྱང་ཆུབ་བསྒྲོག་པ་དང་།
སོ་སོར་ཐར་པ་ཡོངས་སྤྱངས་ནས།
ཐེག་པ་ཆེ་ལ་སྦྱོར་བ་དང་།
སྐྱོབ་པའི་ཐེག་པས་ཆགས་ལ་སོགས།
སྤྱོང་བར་འགྱུར་བར་མིན་ཅེས་འཛིན།
ཕ་རོལ་དག་ཀྱང་འཛིན་འཇུག་དང་།
རང་གི་ཡོན་ཏན་བརྗོད་པ་དང་།
རྙེད་པ་དང་ནི་བཀུར་སྟི་དང་།
ཚིགས་བཅད་རྒྱུ་ཡིས་གཞན་སྐྱོད་དང་།
བདག་ནི་ཟབ་མོ་བཟོད་པའི་ཞེས།
ལོག་པ་ཉིད་ནི་སྒྲུབ་དང་།
དགེ་སྦྱོང་ཆད་པས་གཅོད་འཇུག་དང་།
དཀོན་མཆོག་གསུམ་གྱི་སྙིན་བྱེད་དང་།
སྙིན་ལ་ལེན་པར་བྱེད་པ་དང་།
ཉི་གནས་འདོར་བར་བྱེད་པ་དང་།
ཡང་དག་འཛིན་གི་ལོངས་སྤྱོད་རྣམས།
ཁ་ཏོན་བྱེད་ལ་སྦྱིན་པ་དང་།
འདི་དག་རྩ་བའི་ལྟུང་བ་སྟེ།

Which are causes for the hell realms of living beings.

They should be confessed in dream

Kneeling before Exalted Essence of Space.

IX.   Not offering the three to the Three Jewels;

Following thoughts of desire;

Not respecting one's seniors;

Giving no answer to questions.

X.   Not accepting invitations;

Not taking such things as gold;

Not giving to those who seek teaching;

Disdaining the immoral.

XI.   Not training for the sake of others' faith;

Doing too little for the good of living beings;

With compassion there is no non-virtue;

Readily accepting a wrong livelihood.

XII. Getting very excited through distraction;

Thinking to travel only in cyclic existence;

Failing to prevent defamation;

Not correcting even [those] with disturbing emotions.

སེམས་ཅན་དམྱལ་བ་ཆེན་པོའི་རྒྱུ།
ཀྲི་ལམ་འཐབ་གས་པ་ནས་སྟིང་པོའི།
མདུན་དུ་འདུག་སྟེ་བཤགས་པར་བྱ།   དགོ་པོ།།

^९ དགོན་མཆོག་གསུམ་ལ་གསུམ་མི་མཆོད།
འདོད་པའི་སེམས་ཀྱི་རྫས་སུ་འཛུག
ཀུན་པ་རྣམས་ལ་གུས་མི་བྱེད།
ངིས་པ་ལ་ནི་ལན་མི་འདེབས།

^{१०} མགྲོན་པོ་བདག་གིར་མི་བྱེད་ཅིང་།
གསེར་ལ་སོགས་པ་ཡིན་མི་བྱེད།
ཆོས་འདོད་པ་ལ་སྦྱིན་མི་བྱེད།
ཚུལ་ཁྲིམས་འཆལ་རྣམས་ཡལ་བར་འདོར།

^{११} ཕ་རོལ་དད་ཕྱིར་སློབ་མི་བྱེད།
སེམས་ཅན་དོན་ལ་བྲུ་བ་ཆུང་།
སྙིང་བརྩེར་བཅས་ན་མི་དགེ་མེད།
འཚོ་བ་ལོག་པ་དང་དུ་ལེན།

^{१२} འཕྱར་ནས་རབ་ཏུ་རྒོད་ལ་སོགས།
འཁོར་བ་གཅིག་པུ་བགྲོད་པར་སེམས།
གྲགས་པ་མ་ཡིན་མི་སྤྱོངས་པ།
ཉིན་མོངས་བཅས་ཀྱང་འཆོས་མི་བྱེད།

XIII.   Abuse in return for abuse, and so forth;

Ignoring those who are angry;

Disregarding another's excuses;

Following thoughts of anger.

XIV.   Gathering followers out of desire for reward and respect;

Not getting rid of laziness and so forth;

Indulging in gossip with passion;

Not seeking the object of meditative stabilization.

XV.   Not eliminating the hindrances to concentration;

Appreciating the taste of concentration;

Giving up the Hearer Vehicle;

Effort in that, despite having one's own method.

XVI.   Without effort except for non-Buddhist treatises;

Making effort and also liking them;

Rejecting the Great Vehicle;

Praising oneself or disparaging others.

XVII.   Not to go for the teachings;

Deprecating them and relying upon the letter;

༡༣   གཞི་ལ་ལན་དུ་གཞི་ལ་སོགས།
       ཁྲིམས་པ་རྣམས་ནི་ཡལ་བས་འཛིག
       ཕ་རོལ་ཞད་ཀྱིས་བཆགས་པ་སྦྱིང་།
       ཁྲི་བའི་སེམས་ཀྱི་རྗེས་སུ་འཇུག

༡༤   བསྐྱེན་བགྱུར་འདོད་ཕྱིར་འཕོར་རྣམས་སྟུད།
       ལེ་ལོ་ལ་སོགས་སེལ་མི་བྱེད།
       ཆགས་པས་བྲེ་མོའི་གཏམ་ལ་བརྗེན།
       ཏིང་ངེ་འཛིན་གྱི་དོན་མི་ཚོལ།

༡༥   བསམ་གཏན་སྐྱབ་པ་སྦྱོང་མི་བྱེད།
       བསམ་གཏན་རོ་ལ་ཡོན་ཏན་ལྟ།
       ཉན་ཐོས་ཐེག་པ་སྦྱོང་བར་བྱེད།
       རང་ཚུལ་ཡོད་བཞིན་དེ་ལ་བཙོན།

༡༦   བཙོན་མིན་ཕྱི་རོལ་བསྟན་བཅོས་བཙོན།
       བཙོན་པར་བྱས་ཀྱང་དེ་ལ་དགའ།
       ཐེག་པ་ཆེན་པོ་སྤོང་བར་བྱ།
       བདག་ལ་བསྟོད་ཅིང་གཞན་ལ་སྨོད།

༡༧   ཆོས་ཀྱི་དོན་དུ་འགྲོ་མི་བྱེད།
       དེ་ལ་སྐྱོད་ཅིང་ཡི་གི་བརྗེད།

Not being a friend in need;

Refusing to serve the sick.

XVIII. Not removing suffering;

Not teaching the careless what is proper;

Not repaying a good deed;

Not assuaging others' grief.

XIX.   Not giving to those who want wealth;

Not working for the welfare of followers;

Not conforming to others' ideas;

Not speaking in praise of good qualities.

XX.   Not punishing to fit the circumstances;

Not using miraculous feats to threaten and so forth.

There is no fault if one who has compassion,

Is loving and has a virtuous mind.

དགོས་པའི་འགྲོགས་སུ་འགྲོ་མི་བྱེད། །
ནད་པའི་རིམ་གྲོ་བྱ་བ་སྤོང་། །

༡༥   སྡུག་བསྔལ་སེལ་བར་མི་བྱེད་པ། །
བག་མེད་རྣམས་ལ་རིགས་མི་སྟོན། །
བྱམས་ལ་ལན་དུ་ཕན་མི་འདོགས། །
གཞན་གྱི་ཁྱུ་རྫན་བསངད་མི་བྱེད། །

༡༩   ནོར་འདོད་པ་ལ་སྦྱིན་མི་བྱེད། །
འཁོར་རྣམས་ཀྱི་ཉེ་དོན་མི་བྱེད། །
གཞན་གྱི་བློ་དང་མཐུན་མི་འཇུག །
ཨོན་ཏན་བསྔགས་པ་སྨྲ་མི་བྱེད། །

༣༠   རྐྱེན་དུ་འཚལ་བར་ཚར་མི་གཅོད། །
ཧྭ་འཕྲུལ་སྟེག་ལ་སོགས་མི་བྱེད། །
སྲིད་རྗེས་ལྱུན་ཞིང་བྱམས་ཕྱིར་དང་། །
སེམས་དགོ་བ་ལ་ཉེས་པ་མེད། །

བྱང་ཆུབ་སེམས་དཔའི་སྡོམ་པ་ཉི་ཤུ་པ།
སློབ་དཔོན་ཆེན་དུ་གོ་མིས་མཛད་པ་རྫོགས་སོ། །

Appendix 1

A Traditional Biography of Chandragomin[1]

In the east of India, in Varendra, lived a scholar who had a vision of Avalokiteshvara. He debated with a non-Buddhist master and defeated him. This master protested that he had been defeated simply because of the other's intellectual prowess and that the scholar had failed to convince him of the existence of past and future lives because he had not produced any evidence.

The scholar asked the king and others to act as witnesses and requested them to put a mark on his forehead, saying that he would provide proof of rebirth. They made an incision in his forehead and colored it with vermilion. He then swallowed a pearl which caused him to die instantly and his corpse was placed in a covered copper vat which was sealed by the king.

He took birth as the son of a scholar named Visheshaka belonging to the warrior caste. His forehead showed a vermilion mark and in his mouth they found a pearl. When the king and his court examined the corpse they discovered that both the vermilion mark and the pearl were gone. This convinced the non-Buddhist master regarding the existence of past and future lives.

Immediately after his birth, the child, who was given the name Chandra, bowed down before his mother and said, "I hope you didn't suffer too much." His mother was so shocked that she told him not to speak, which is what he did for seven years and everyone thought that he would remain dumb.

At that time a non-Buddhist wrote a difficult treatise in verse refuting Buddhist views. Copies of it were given to kings and scholars and in this way a copy reached Visheshaka's house. Visheshaka could hardly understand its meaning, never mind refute it. He left it lying in the house when he went out to do some work. Chandra, who was seven at the time, saw it and had no difficulty at all explaining and refuting it in the form of a short gloss and some verses.

When Visheshaka returned and found what Chandra had written, he asked his wife if anyone had come to visit. She said no visitors had called but that the dumb boy had been reading and writing. His father questioned him but he did not speak until his mother gave him permission. The next day a debate was arranged between the non-Buddhist and Chandra. Chandra was declared victorious and received a generous reward. After this he taught himself grammar and logic, acquired other forms of knowledge and became famous for his learning. He had visions of Avalokiteshvara and Tara and wrote treatises on medicine, composition, the fine arts and grammar, in which he was an expert.

He married a princess called Tara and received a province from the king, but once when he heard a female maidservant addressing the princess as Tara, he felt it was improper to live a conjugal life with someone who bore the name of a deity and decided to leave for another place. The king came to know of it and ordered that Chandra should be put in a box and thrown into the Ganges if he refused to live with the princess. Chandra prayed fervently to Tara for help and the box drifted to an island. It is said that the island, big enough for seven thousand villages, was miraculously created and that it still exists.

While on the island, he set up stone images of Avalokiteshvara and Tara and slowly more and more fishermen and other people came to live there until their dwellings formed a city. Avalokiteshvara instructed Chandra to take the lay person's vow and to abstain from sexual activity. To indicate this, "gomin" was added to his former name, Chandra.

Merchants took him to Sinhala, probably present-day Sri Lanka, where leprosy was rife. Chandragomin build a temple there and the disease was miraculously wiped out. Chandragomin gave Mahayana teachings, composed grammatical works and with wealth given to him by the spirit ruler of the place, built many centers of education. He widely disseminated knowledge of the fine arts, medicine and other branches of learning and contributed greatly to the welfare of the inhabitants of that island.

In those days, at Nalanda,[2] scholars capable of debating with non-Buddhists taught and debated outside Nalanda's walls, whereas those who were less skilled did so within. When Chandragomin arrived there from the south, Chandrakirti was teaching outside the walls of the great monastic university and Chandragomin stood nearby to listen. Usually those who wanted to challenge the speaker stood, so when Chandrakirti caught sight of Chandragomin, he wondered whether this was an opponent who wished to challenge him in debate. He asked from where he had come and Chandragomin replied that he had come from the south. Chandrakirti then questioned him about what he knew and was satisfied by the reply he received. Though Chandragomin's words did not express pride they implied that he knew all about grammar, sutra and tantra. Chandrakirti wondered whether this was Chandragomin and asked his name.

Then Chandrakirti said that a great scholar should not appear as unexpectedly as a flash of lightning but should be properly welcomed by the spiritual community. Chandragomin replied that he was only a holder of the lay person's vow and so could surely not be welcomed formally by the ordained community. However Chandrakirti thought of a way. He said that they would accompany a statue of Manjushri to the monastery and that Chandragomin should fan the image. The spiritual community would turn out to welcome Manjushri and this would be perfectly acceptable in the eyes of the common people.

He arranged for three chariots, and the statue of Manjushri was placed in the central one. Chandrakirti fanned the statue from the chariot on the right and Chandragomin from the one on the left. The members of the spiritual community awaited them in front of the monastery. Many people came to watch. To Chandragomin the statue appeared as Manjushri himself and he began to praise him. Everyone saw the head of the statue turn in his direction and as they pointed it out to each other the image froze. Later this image was known as the "Exalted one with his head turned to the left." At that moment Chandragomin's charioteer failed to restrain his horse and his chariot moved ahead of Chandrakirti's. Thinking this a mark of Chandragomin's disrespect and ignorance, Chandrakirti determined to debate with him.

In the debate which followed Chandragomin held the view of Asanga and defended the Chittamatrin position. Following the view of Nagarjuna, as interpreted by Buddhapalita, Chandrakirti defended the position that nothing has intrinsic existence. Their debate continued for seven years and each time they met there were many people present to witness their disputation.

Once towards the end of that debate the following happened. At night Chandragomin used to sit in the temple of Avalokiteshvara, who provided him with answers to the arguments which Chandrakirti had raised during the day. Next morning Chandragomin would offer these answers which Chandrakirti could not refute. Chandrakirti began to get suspicious after several months passed in this way. One day he followed Chandragomin and from outside the temple, he overheard Avalokiteshvara teaching Chandragomin. Chandrakirti opened the door and inquired of Avalokiteshvara whether he was not showing partiality by favoring Chandragomin in this way. At that moment Avalokiteshvara turned back into a statue and his finger remained raised. He had just been saying, "If he says that, then you must say this...." The statue became known as "Avalokiteshvara with his forefinger raised." In this way the debate came to an end.

As a result of Chandrakirti's earnest prayers Avalokiteshvara told him in a dream, "You are already blessed by Manjushri and don't need my blessings, so I have bestowed them on Chandragomin."

Chandragomin stayed on at Nalanda. While there he came across an excellent treatise on grammar written by Chandrakirti. Realizing this was much more poetic than his own, he threw the treatise he had written into a well. But Tara appeared to him and told him that he had written his treatise with the intention to benefit others while Chandrakirti had written his with pride in his scholarship and that, therefore, long after Chandrakirti's work had been forgotten, Chandragomin's would continue to be of use to many people. Saying this she told him to retrieve his book from the well. After this incident those who drank from the well were instantly filled with wisdom.

Chandragomin continued to write many books on the fine arts, grammar, logic, medicine, dramaturgy, poetics and astronomy, and he compiled a dictionary. He taught these subjects extensively till one day Tara appeared to him and told him not to teach secular knowledge but to concentrate on the teachings of the Buddha. His *Twenty Verses on the Bodhisattva Vow* was widely studied by Maha- yana scholars who came after him.

Once there was an old woman who had a beautiful daughter. As she had no money for her daughter's wedding, she went from place to place begging until eventually she reached Nalanda. Hav- ing heard that the scholar Chandrakirti was famous and thinking he might have great wealth, she went to beg from him. Chandrakirti told her that he was a simple monk and did not have many posses- sions. What money he had was dedicated to the temples and to the spiritual community. He suggested that she should try Chandra- gomin, who lived nearby.

The old woman went to beg from him but he told her that though he was a lay person, he had only the clothes he was wearing. There was a painting of Tara on the wall. Moved by compassion for the old woman, Chandragomin prayed to Tara with tears in his eyes. Tara came to life and took off her ornaments which were made of precious jewels. She gave them to Chandragomin who joyfully handed them to the old woman. The old woman was happy and amazed at her good fortune. This image of Tara came to be known as the "Tara without ornaments." The empty places where the or- naments had been were aflame.

Eventually Chandragomin resolved to go to Potala[3] and sailed to the island of Dhanashri. A powerful naga, who had written a verbose, repetitive and incomplete commentary on a famous gram- mar and whom Chandragomin had offended by his sharp criti- cism of it, caused a storm which was so violent that the ship was in danger of sinking. Then a voice was heard from the deep saying, "Throw out Chandragomin." But when Chandragomin prayed to Tara, she and her four attendants came flying there on the back of a *garuda*.[4] The nagas fled in terror and the ship arrived safely in Dhanashri. There Chandragomin made offerings to Avalokitesh- vara and Tara and built a hundred temples for each. Eventually he went to Potala hill and is said still to be living there without having given up his mortal body.

Appendix 2

The Seven-part Practice

from The King of Prayers, The Prayer of Noble Conduct

I pay homage to the youthful noble Manjushri!

1. I pay homage with body, speech and mind
   To all Buddhas, past, present and future,
   To all those lions amongst humans, as many
   As there are in the worlds of the ten directions.

2. Through the power of this prayer of noble conduct,
   In my mind's eye I see all those Victorious Ones.
   With as many bodies as there are atoms in the worlds,
   I bow to them all, the Victorious Ones.

3. On every atom, amidst Bodhisattvas,
   Are as many Buddhas as there are atoms,
   And similarly I imagine the whole
   Sphere of phenomena filled with Buddhas.

4.   With an inexhaustible ocean of praise,
      Through oceans of sound made with the organs of speech,
      I speak of the qualities of the Victorious
      And praise all those who have gone to bliss.

5.   With the finest flowers and finest garlands,
      With the sweetest music, best unguents and best parasols,
      With the best butterlamps and the finest incense,
      I make offerings to all those Victorious Ones.

6.   With fine clothes and the best fragrances,
      Aromatic powders heaped high as the king of mountains,
      All arranged in the most excellent fashion,
      I make offerings to those Victorious Ones.

7.   I imagine giving all the Victorious Ones
      The most extensive and unsurpassable offerings.
      Through the power of faith in noble conduct
      I bow and make offerings to all Victorious Ones.

8.   Whatever wrong actions I have created
      With my body, my speech and with my mind,
      Driven by desire, anger and confusion,
      Each of these I openly acknowledge.

9.   I rejoice in the merit of the Victorious Ones
      And of Bodhisattvas in the ten directions,
      Of Solitary Realizers, trainees and the perfected
      And in that of all living beings.

10. I urge those protectors who have just gained
Buddhahood—enlightenment without obstruction,
Who are lamps for the worlds in the ten directions,
To turn the unsurpassable wheel of the teachings.

11. With folded hands I request those who wish
To display the passing into parinirvana,
To remain for the benefit and joy of living beings
For as many aeons as the worlds have atoms.

12. I dedicate the slight merit I have created
Through reverence, offerings and confession,
Through rejoicing, exhorting and through requesting,
To the attainment of highest enlightenment.

Translated by Ruth Sonam, Dharamsala, January 1997

Appendix 3

The Eighteen Downfalls and Forty-six Faulty Actions

The Eighteen Transgressions of the Bodhisattva Vow which are Downfalls

1. Praising oneself or disparaging others
2. Not giving teachings or wealth
3. Not heeding the confession of others or striking them in anger
4. Rejecting the Great Vehicle or giving a counterfeit of the excellent teachings
5. Robbing what belongs to the Three Jewels
6. Rejecting the teachings
7. Taking away the robes of ordained people
8. Committing any of the five heinous crimes
9. Holding wrong views
10. Destroying towns and so forth
11. Explaining emptiness to the unprepared
12. Encouraging another to give up the intention to attain complete enlightenment
13. Encouraging another to give up the individual liberation vow
14. Disparaging the Hearer Vehicle
15. Telling a lie about the profound
16. Taking what has been offered to the Three Jewels

17. Following bad discipline
18. Giving up the altruistic intention

The Forty-six Transgressions which are Faulty Actions

1. Not making offerings to the Three Jewels through physical homage, praise and faith
2. Following thoughts of desire
3. Not respecting one's seniors
4. Giving no answer to questions
5. Not accepting invitations
6. Not taking such things as gold
7. Not giving to those who seek teachings
8. Disdaining the immoral
9. Not training for the sake of others' faith
10. Doing too little for the good of living beings
11. Not doing out of compassion what is otherwise non-virtuous
12. Readily accepting a wrong livelihood
13. Getting very excited through distraction
14. Thinking to travel only in cyclic existence
15. Failing to prevent defamation
16. Not correcting even those with disturbing emotions
17. Abuse in return for abuse, and so forth
18. Ignoring those who are angry
19. Disregarding another's excuses
20. Following thoughts of anger
21. Gathering followers out of desire for reward and respect
22. Not getting rid of laziness and so forth
23. Indulging in gossip with passion
24. Not seeking the object of meditative stabilization
25. Not eliminating the hindrances to concentration
26. Appreciating the taste of concentration
27. Giving up the Hearer Vehicle

28. Effort in that, despite having one's own method
29. Without effort except for non-Buddhist treatises
30. Making effort and also liking them
31. Rejecting the Great Vehicle
32. Praising oneself or disparaging others
33. Not going for the teachings
34. Deprecating them and relying upon the letter
35. Not being a friend in need
36. Refusing to serve the sick
37. Not removing suffering
38. Not teaching the careless what is proper
39. Not repaying a good deed
40. Not assuaging others' grief
41. Not giving to those who want wealth
42. Not working for the welfare of followers
43. Not conforming to others' ideas
44. Not speaking in praise of good qualities
45. Not punishing to fit the circumstances
46. Not using miraculous feats to threaten and so forth

The Four Binding Factors

1. Not regarding the action as faulty
2. Not giving up the desire to do it
3. Enjoying and delighting in it
4. Being shameless and unembarrassed

Notes

ABBREVIATION

P: *Tibetan Tripiṭaka* (Tokyo-Kyoto: Tibetan Tripitaka Research Foundation, 1956)

CHAPTER 1: THE HEART OF MAHAYANA PRACTICE

1. People are motivated by different intentions when they practice the Buddha's teachings. From a Buddhist point of view practice of the teachings is considered authentic when it is motivated at least by the wish to gain a good rebirth. A practitioner of the initial level or most limited capacity (*skye bu chung ngu*) engages in practices which make this possible. A practitioner of the intermediate level (*skye bu 'bring*) is concerned with personal liberation from all rebirth within cyclic existence as a result of actions underlain by disturbing attitudes and emotions, and engages in practices which lead to such freedom. A practitioner of the highest level or great capacity (*skye bu chen po*) is motivated by the altruistic intention to become enlightened for the sake of all living beings (*byang chub sems*) and does what is necessary to become a fully enlightened Buddha. Even if from the outset we are motivated by the wish to become fully enlightened in order to help others in the most effective way, we must still gain the insights associated with the initial and intermediate levels, since these insights form the foundation for the practices that are unique to the Great Vehicle.

2. *Lamp for the Path to Enlightenment (Bodhipathapradipa, Byang chub lam gyi sgron ma,* P5343, Vol. 103) is the forerunner of the subsequent *lam rim* literature, which explains the stages of the path to enlightenment with strong emphasis on practice. Atisha (known as Jo bo rje in Tibetan, 982-1054) was born into a royal family probably in what is now Bengal. Owing to his parents' opposition he had difficulty disengaging himself from royal life but eventually, after a number of attempts, he succeeded and became ordained. He studied with one hundred and fifty-seven spiritual masters but was always very moved when he recalled Dharmakirti of Suvarnadvipa, the master of the Golden Isles. Atisha made a perilous thirteen-month sea journey to Indonesia to study with this master, with whom he remained for twelve years and to whom he attributed his development of the altruistic intention. After his return to India he lived in the monastic university of Vikramashila from where he was invited to Tibet. Atisha's visit to Tibet, where he remained from 1042 until his death, had a profound influence on the course of Buddhism there. English translation and commentary: Geshe Sonam Rinchen and Ruth Sonam, *Atisha's Lamp for the Path to Enlightenment* (Ithaca, New York: Snow Lion Publications, 1997).

3. The four noble truths (*'phags pa'i bden pa bzhi*) are true suffering (*sdug bsngal bden pa*), true sources of suffering (*kun 'byung bden pa*), true cessation (*'gog pa'i bden pa*) and true paths (*lam gyi bden pa*).

4. Hearers (*snyan thos*) and Solitary Realizers (*rang sangs rgyas*) are intent on gaining personal liberation. They are practitioners of the Hinayana or Lesser Vehicle (*theg dman pa*), so called because their objective is limited to their own well-being. Practitioners of the Mahayana or Great Vehicle (*theg chen pa*), which consists of the Perfection Vehicle (*pha rol tu chin pa'i theg pa*) and the Secret Mantra Vehicle (*gsang sngags kyi theg pa*), aspire to attain complete enlightenment (*rdzogs pa'i byang chub*) for the sake of all beings and therefore have a much greater objective. Solitary Realizers accumulate more merit over a longer period than Hearers and do not depend upon the instructions of a spiritual teacher in their last rebirth before they attain liberation and become Foe Destroyers (*dgra bcom pa*).

5. Aung San Suu Kyi in her speech in Kachin State, Burma, 27 April 1989, says, "To live the full life one must have the courage to bear the responsibility of the needs of others—one must want to bear

this responsibility." See *Freedom from Fear* (New York: Penguin Books, 1991).

6. The Indian master Shantideva (Zhi ba lha) lived in the monastic university of Nalanda during the eighth century. To others he appeared quite unaccomplished and they said he only knew three things: how to eat, sleep and defecate. In an attempt to humiliate him he was designated to teach before a large gathering. To everyone's amazement he showed himself to be a very great master by teaching his guide to the Bodhisattva way of life, the *Way of the Bodhisattva* (*Bodhisattvacaryāvatāra, Byang chub sems dpa'i spyod pa la 'jug pa*, P5272, Vol. 99), and by displaying miraculous feats. English translations: *A Guide to the Bodhisattva's Way of Life*, Stephen Batchelor, trans. (Dharamsala: Library of Tibetan Works and Archives, 1979); *The Bodhicaryāvatāra*, Kate Crosby and Andrew Skilton, trans. (Oxford: Oxford University Press, 1995); *A Guide to the Bodhisattva Way of Life*, Vesna A. Wallace and B. Alan Wallace, trans. (Ithaca: Snow Lion Publications, 1997); *The Way of the Bodhisattva*, Padmakara Translation Group, trans. (Boston: Shambhala Publications, 1997). Verses quoted in this book are taken from the latter translation.

7. The format of Tsongkhapa's exhaustive *Great Exposition of the Stages of the Path* (*Lam rim chen mo*, P6001, Vol. 152) and of his other works on the stages of the path was directly inspired by Atisha's practice-oriented *Lamp for the Path to Enlightenment*.

8. In tantra the stage of generation (*bskyed rim*) is practiced to overcome ordinary appearances and one's clinging to them. Ordinary appearances are counteracted by imagining oneself as the deity and one's surroundings as the celestial mansion and other components of the mandala. One's clinging to such ordinary appearances is countered by strong identification with the deity. Practices during the stage of completion (*rdzogs rim*) involve focusing intense attention on the energy channels, energy winds and drops of the subtle body, particularly at the different centers, to generate great bliss. This blissful awareness is eventually used to apprehend emptiness and to produce the illusory body (*sgyu lus*).

9. The five paths are the path of accumulation (*tshogs lam*), the path of preparation (*sbyor lam*), the path of seeing (*mthong lam*), the path of meditation (*sgom lam*) and the path of no more learning (*mi slob*

lam). One enters the Mahayana path of accumulation and becomes a Bodhisattva when the altruistic intention is spontaneously and constantly present. At this point one begins to accumulate the great stores of merit and insight necessary for the attainment of enlightenment. The path of preparation, marked by the union of a calmly abiding mind and special insight focusing on emptiness, prepares one for the direct perception of reality. When this experience of reality is achieved, one becomes an exalted being, attains the path of seeing and the first Bodhisattva stage. On the path of meditation the Mahayana practitioner gains ever-increasing familiarity with the direct perception of emptiness and practices the perfections, eliminating more and more subtle obstructions to enlightenment. When all of these have been removed, one attains the path of no more learning and becomes an enlightened being.

10. The Indian master Nagarjuna (Klu sgrub, first to second century) was the trailblazer who established the Madhyamika system of philosophical tenets. Nagarjuna's *Precious Garland of Advice for the King* (*Rājaparikathāratnāvalī, rGyal po la gtam bya ba rin po che'i phreng ba*, P5658, Vol. 129) explains both the extensive and profound paths to enlightenment, emphasizing that the root of peerless enlightenment is the combination of the altruistic intention and the exalted understanding of reality. Like his *Letter to a Friend* (*Suhṛllekha, bShes pa'i spring yig*, P5682, Vol. 129), it is addressed to his royal friend, a king of the Satavahana dynasty. The *Precious Garland* contains very practical advice, still relevant today, on how to govern in accordance with the Buddha's teaching. English translation: Jeffrey Hopkins, in *The Precious Garland and the Song of the Four Mindfulnesses*, by Nagarjuna and the Seventh Dalai Lama (New York: Harper and Row, 1975); revised in *Buddhist Advice for Living and Liberation: Nāgārjuna's Precious Garland* (Ithaca: Snow Lion Publications, 1998).

11. The five major fields of knowledge are the arts and crafts (*bzo rig pa*), medicine (*gso ba rig pa*), grammar (*sgra rig pa*), logic (*gtan tshigs rig pa*) and Buddhist philosophy (*nang don rig pa*).

12. Drubkang Gelek Gyatso (sGrub khang dGe legs rgya mtsho, 1641-1713) spent more than fifty years meditating on a mountain top behind Sera Monastery not far from Lhasa in central Tibet. One of his most important teachers was Rengo Atsara (Re sgo a tsa ra).

Phurchok Ngawang Jampa (Phur lchog Ngag dbang byams pa, 1682-1762) was one of Drubkang Gelek Gyatso's main disciples.

13. *Stories of The Buddha's Former Lives (Jātakanidāna, sKyes rab kyi gleng gzhi)*, P748, Vol. 21. A collection of these stories, often referred to as the Jataka Tales in English (*Jātakamālā, sKyes rab kyi rgyud*, P5650, Vol. 128) is attributed to Ashvaghosha (rTa dbyangs), also known as Aryashura, who is said to have converted to Buddhism as a result of debating with Aryadeva. For a selection of these stories, see *The Jātakamālā*, translated by J.S. Speyer (Delhi: Motilal Banarsidass, 1971).

14. A functional thing (*ngos po*), produced by causes and conditions, in turn produces results. Thus Drubkang Gelek Gyatso was reassuring his teacher that he meant to assemble the necessary causes and conditions within himself that would give rise to the altruistic intention and that the altruistic intention would change him.

15. It is said that of the eighty-four thousand different teachings, twenty-one thousand were intended to counteract desire, greed, attachment and other associated disturbing emotions; twenty-one thousand were intended as antidotes to anger, hatred, hostility and so forth; twenty-one thousand were intended as counteractions to confusion, ignorance and the like; and a final twenty-one thousand were intended to counteract these three poisons together, which are the root of all other disturbing emotions and the source of all physical sickness.

16. The Kadampa (bKa' gdams pa) tradition was founded by Dromtön Gyelway Jungnay ('Brom ston rGyal ba'i 'byung gnas, 1004-1064), a lay practitioner and the main Tibetan disciple of the Indian master Atisha. The Kadampa masters were known for their down-to-earth approach to practice, which they presented according to the three levels of capacity explained in Atisha's *Lamp for the Path to Enlightenment*. In public they laid great emphasis on the practice of sutra and kept their personal practice of tantra hidden. They regarded all of the Buddha's words (*bka'*) as actual instructions (*gdams*) for practice.

17. Ajatashatru (Ma skyes dgra) was the king of Magadha, part of the present Indian state of Bihar. He ruled during the last eight years of the Buddha's life and for the following twenty-four years.

He was the son of Bimbisara (gZugs can snying po), who had become a follower of the Buddha at the age of thirty, after hearing him teach. Ajatashatru murdered his father but was able to purify himself of this terrible deed and eventually became a Foe Destroyer. He acted as benefactor when the first compilation of the Buddha's teachings was made under the auspices of Mahakashyapa ('Od srung) soon after the Buddha had passed away.

18. The *Gandavyuha Sutra* (*Gaṇḍavyūhasūtra, sDong po bkod pa'i mdo, also known as sDong po rgyan pa'i mdo*, P761, Vol. 26) is part of the *Avatamsaka Sutra* (*Buddhāvataṃsakasūtra, Sangs rgyas phal po che shes bya ba shin tu rgyas pa chen po'i mdo*, P761, Vols. 25-26, also known as *mDo sde phal po che*). English translation: Thomas Cleary, *The Flower Ornament Scripture*, Vols. 1-3 (Boston: Shambhala Publications, 1986). This statement reads: *byang chub kyi sems nyid sangs rgyas kyi chos thams cad kyi sa bon lta bu'o.*

19. The Indian Buddhist master Asanga (Thogs med), who lived in the fourth century, was a trailblazer in establishing the Chittamatrin (Sems tsam pa) system of philosophical tenets, although he himself is said to have held the Prasangika-Madhyamika (dBu ma thal 'gyur pa) philosophical view.

According to the traditional account Asanga was so moved by the sight of the dying bitch that he decided to remove the maggots, but realizing that they would die if he tried to do this with his hands, he made a wound on his leg in which to place them and, closing his eyes, leaned forward to pick up the maggots with his tongue. To his surprise his tongue did not encounter the bitch's flesh and when he opened his eyes he saw neither the bitch nor the maggots but Maitreya (rJe btsun Byams pa), who told him that he had been present the whole time that Asanga had stayed in the cave meditating. Only now, through the power of Asanga's compassion, had the obstructions which prevented him from seeing Maitreya been removed. Asanga was so joyful, he hoisted Maitreya onto his shoulders and carried him triumphantly into the nearby town. Nobody noticed anything except for an old woman who saw him carrying a dog.

When the Buddha Shakyamuni came to our world from the Tushita pure land, Maitreya took over as its spiritual ruler. He will eventually manifest in this world as the next Buddha and display the deeds of a supreme emanation body (*mchog gi sprul sku*). It is said that if one hears and thinks about the five treatises which he revealed to Asanga, one will be reborn in the Tushita pure land. In Tibet many of the largest statues were of Maitreya, who is represented sitting on a throne with his feet on the ground, ready to rise and come into the world. Just as Avalokiteshvara is the embodiment of compassion, Maitreya is the embodiment of love.

20. Je Monlam Pelwa (rJe sMon lam dpal ba, 1414-1490) was the eighth Ganden Throne-holder, the highest position within the Gelugpa hierarchy held only by those who have distinguished themselves as scholars. They represent Je Tsongkhapa (Tsong kha pa Blo bzang grags pa, 1357-1419), born in Amdo (A mdo), who was a great reformer, dedicated practitioner, prolific writer and the founder of Ganden Monastery (dGa' ldan rnam par rgyal ba'i gling) in 1409, the first of the monastic universities of the new Kadampa (bKa' gdams gsar ma) or Gelugpa (dGe lugs pa) tradition.

21. In Lhasa the great prayer festival (*smon lam*) was held for twenty-one days after the lunar new year (*lo gsar*), normally occurring in February or March.

22. There are four kinds of universal monarchs (*'khor los sgyur ba'i rgyal po*) whose emblems are a gold, silver, copper and iron wheel respectively to symbolize the difference in the extent of their power. The four great kings (*rgyal chen bzhi*) who protect the cardinal points are Yulkor Sung (Yul 'khor srung) in the east, Pakyepo ('Phags skyes po) in the south, Jenmisang (sPyan mi bzang) in the west and Namtösey (rNam thos sras) in the north.

23. The mind's nature is clear light (*'od gsal ba*) in two ways. Conventionally the mind is clear and cognizant (*gsal zhing rig pa*). It is often compared to a clean mirror in which anything can be reflected. This emphasizes the fact that the disturbing emotions are not an integral part of it but a temporary pollutant. Ultimately the nature of the mind is clear light in that it is empty of true existence.

24. The Perfection of Wisdom sutras were taught by the Buddha at Vulture's Peak outside Rajgir. As an act of homage to the teaching he was about to give he prepared his own seat. The explicit subject-matter (*dngos don*) of these sutras consists of the stages of the profound paths of practice regarding the nature of reality, the emptiness of intrinsic existence of all phenomena, and how this understanding is used to eliminate the obstructions to liberation and to

knowledge of all phenomena. The hidden subject-matter (*sbas don*) consists of the stages of the extensive paths of practice, namely everything which constitutes the development of skillful means. Normally a hidden subject-matter is found only in the tantras, while sutras may have an explicit (*dngos don*) and implicit subject-matter (*shugs don*). The fact that the Perfection of Wisdom sutras have a hidden subject-matter places them close to the tantras regarding the subtlety of their content. They contain much that can only be understood with the help of a spiritual teacher's instructions. Of the many versions of these sutras the best known in the Tibetan canon are those consisting of a hundred thousand verses, twenty thousand verses, eight thousand verses and the *Heart Sutra* (*Bhagavatīprajñāpāramitāhṛdayasūtra, bCom ldan 'das ma shes rab kyi pha rol tu phyin pa'i snying po'i mdo*, P160, Vol. 6), the most condensed Perfection of Wisdom sutra.

25. A chapter of the *Eight Thousand Verse Perfection of Wisdom Sutra* (*Aṣṭasāhasrikāprajñāpāramitāsūtra, Shes rab kyi pha rol tu phyin pa rgyad stong pa*, P732, Vols. 19-20) is devoted to the story of the Bodhisattva Sadaprarudita, the Ever-Weeping Bodhisattva, who had a deep longing to gain perfect wisdom and to become a light for others.

One day he heard a voice from the sky which told him to give up everything that might bind him to cyclic existence and to go eastwards if he wished to hear teachings on the perfection of wisdom. He set out on his journey with enthusiasm but after some time realized that he had no idea where he was going. He wept at his own stupidity and resolved to stay in the same place until the voice spoke to him again. This time an enlightened being appeared to him and reassured him that he had done the right thing. He told Sadaprarudita to go the city of Ghandavati where he would find a magnificent palace in which lived the Bodhisattva Dharmodgata. Dharmodgata was about to teach on the perfection of wisdom to a great gathering of humans and gods.

Sadaprarudita was ecstatic when he heard this but now he had the problem of what to offer to this great teacher when he requested permission to attend the teachings. As he was very poor and had no good possessions he decided to sell himself. On reaching the next town he offered himself for sale but no one took any notice of him. Sadaprarudita felt completely discouraged. Seeing this, one of the gods, who wished to test him, took the form of a Brahmin. He said he didn't need Sadaprarudita but that what he wanted was a human heart, some human blood and some marrow for a certain ritual he wished to perform. Without hesitating, Sadaprarudita offered himself. The Brahmin took out a sharp knife, cut Sadaprarudita's arm and began to draw blood.

When he was preparing to pierce Sadaprarudita's thigh in order to extract marrow from the bone, the daughter of a wealthy family, who had been watching from the window of her house, could not bear it any longer and came to the Brahmin to find out what was happening. As soon as she heard why Sadaprarudita was sacrificing himself, she promised that he could have whatever he needed to offer to his teacher. The god then resumed his proper form and explained that he had merely been testing Sadaprarudita's resolve. He asked how he could recompense Sadaprarudita, to which the latter immediately replied, "Give me enlightenment!" The god had to confess that he could not do this and so Sadaprarudita requested him to restore his body to its former condition.

The daughter of the wealthy family took Sadaprarudita to her home, where he was given many rich offerings, and her family were so impressed with his devotion that they allowed her to accompany him to Gandhavati together with five hundred attendant maidens. They found Dharmodgata and with great joy gave him their gifts. After teaching Sadaprarudita and his companions about the true nature of reality, Dharmodgata went into his palace and remained in deep absorption for seven years.

During those seven long years Sadaprarudita lived austerely as he waited anxiously for his teacher to reappear. When the time came for Dharmodgata to arise from meditation, Sadaprarudita tried to find water to sprinkle on the ground to settle the dust, but there was at that time a great drought. He was sprinkling his own blood on the ground, when the god who had tested him once more appeared and gave him everything that was necessary to prepare and adorn the place. This time when Dharmodgata taught, Sadaprarudita gained countless profound insights and inconceivable wisdom.

26. The *Gandavyuha Sutra* tells of the youth Sudhana's quest for wisdom and of his exemplary devotion to the spiritual teachers he met on his pilgrimage and who gave him instruction. Remembering their kindness, Sudhana loses his composure and sheds tears.

He says, "My spiritual teachers have protected me from bad rebirths. They have enabled me to understand the sameness of all phenomena. They have shown me the path to happiness and to unhappiness. They have instructed me in wholly noble deeds. They have shown me the way to the city of omniscience. They accompany me as I journey to the state of omniscience. They have made me enter the oceanic sphere of phenomena. They have shown me the mandala of the assembled exalted ones. They have helped me to increase my white activities," and much more in the same vein.

27. Aryadeva was the spiritual son of Nagarjuna and was active in the monastic university of Nalanda during the first half of the third century. His work *Four Hundred Stanzas on the Yogic Deeds of Bodhisattvas* (*Bodhisattvayogacaryācatuḥśatakaśāstra*, *Byang chub sems dpa'i rnal 'byor spyod pa bzhi brgya pa'i bstan bcos*, P5246, Vol. 95) discusses the distorted ideas and disturbing emotions which prevent true Bodhisattva activity and the attainment of enlightenment. The first eight chapters of this work establish conventional reality, while the second eight establish ultimate reality by refuting various misconceptions regarding, for instance, the person, time, space and matter. English translation: Geshe Sonam Rinchen and Ruth Sonam, *Yogic Deeds of Bodhisattvas: Gyeltsap on Aryadeva's Four Hundred* (Ithaca: Snow Lion Publications, 1994).

28. High status (*mngon mtho*) generally refers to the happiness experienced in good rebirths, while definite goodness (*nges legs*) refers to liberation from cyclic existence. In this passage Nagarjuna explains that it is important first of all to insure that one will take good rebirths and from there one can progress to liberation. Faith and wisdom are essential if one wishes to bring this about. Through faith—particularly conviction regarding the connection between actions and their effects—one will practice the Buddha's teachings and through wisdom one will understand reality. One who does not act in ways that conflict with the teachings because of desire, anger, fear or confusion is said to have faith. Through this one becomes ready to practice the teachings that lead to definite goodness.

29. Enlightened beings have two kinds of bodies, a truth body (*chos sku*) and form bodies (*gzugs sku*). The truth body has two aspects: the nature body (*ngo bo nyid sku*), which is the fundamental nature of omniscient mind, and omniscient mind itself, the wisdom truth body (*ye shes chos sku*). The wisdom truth body is the outcome primarily

of the great store of insight (*ye shes kyi tshogs*) which Buddhas amass while they are Bodhisattvas. Only enlightened beings can perceive the wisdom truth bodies of other enlightened beings. Their form bodies are primarily the result of the great store of merit (*bsod nams kyi tshogs*) which they create while they are Bodhisattvas.

Buddhas manifest two kinds of form bodies for the benefit of others. Their enjoyment body (*longs sku*) is a subtle form body which can only be perceived by exalted Bodhisattvas—those who have attained direct perception of emptiness. Such an enjoyment body gives Mahayana teachings continuously and is adorned with the thirty-two major and eighty minor marks of an enlightened being.

Emanation bodies (*sprul sku*) appear for the benefit of ordinary beings. The supreme emanation body (*mchog gi sprul sku*), in the form of a world teacher, adorned with the thirty-two major and eighty minor marks, like the Buddha Shakyamuni, can only be seen by those with pure karma. Such an emanation body gives teachings of all kinds in accordance with the needs of ordinary beings. Bodhisattvas on the great stage of the path of accumulation can through the meditative stabilization called the "stream of teachings" (*chos rgyun gyi ting nge 'dzin*) receive instruction directly from the supreme emanation body of an enlightened being.

30. The practices of giving (*sbyin pa*), ethical discipline (*tshul khrims*), patience (*bzod pa*), enthusiastic effort (*brtson 'grus*), concentration (*bsam gtan*) and wisdom (*shes rab*) become perfections and practices of Bodhisattvas when the intention underlying them is the altruistic wish to become enlightened for the sake of all living beings. The first five are said to be like a group of blind people who cannot reach the destination of enlightenment without wisdom, which is like their sighted guide. Concentration and wisdom are more easily practiced by ordained people than by lay people. Those who live the life of a householder, however, have plenty of opportunities to practice the first three perfections. Whether lay or ordained it is important to develop enthusiastic effort, which is a delight in virtue.

31. Three kinds of faith are described. They are clear faith (*dang ba'i dad pa*), the faith of conviction (*yid ches kyi dad pa*) and aspiring faith (*mngon 'dod kyi dad pa*). The first focuses on the supreme abilities of an enlightened being with a vivid sense of appreciation which makes our mind bright and clear, dispelling disturbing emotions. Our mind becomes like water in which the mud has settled. The

faith of conviction arises when we gain certainty that practice of the paths will yield the promised insights and that we can rid ourselves of all mental stains. Aspiring faith is the strong wish to practice in order to gain these realizations and to rid ourselves of faults.

CHAPTER 2: HOW TO DEVELOP THE ALTRUISTIC INTENTION

1. The teachings on discipline (*'dul ba'i sde snod*) mainly set forth the training in ethical discipline (*tshul khrims kyi bslab pa*) or conduct (*spyod pa*). Those on knowledge (*mngon pa'i sde snod*) primarily explain the training in wisdom (*shes rab kyi bslab pa*) or the view (*lta ba*), while those on sutra (*mdo sde'i sde snod*) principally explain the training in meditative stabilization (*ting nge 'dzin gyi bslab pa*) or meditation (*sgom pa*).

2. The Indian master Chandrakirti (Zla ba grags pa) was one of the main spiritual heirs of Nagarjuna, whose works on sutra and tantra he elucidated and propagated. He lived in the monastic university of Nalanda during the seventh century and was an accomplished practitioner.

3. The Indian master Kamalashila was a student of Shantarakshita (Zhi ba 'tsho) and participated in a decisive debate with a Chinese monk identified as Hva-shang Mahayana. This debate was held in Tibet in 792 at Samye Monastery (bSam yas) and, according to Tibetan sources, the outcome definitively settled that Buddhism in Tibet would follow the Indian rather than the Chinese model.

4. The seven cause and effect instructions (*rgyu 'bras man ngag bdun*) consist of recognizing all living beings as our mothers (*mar shes*), remembering their kindness (*drin dran*), cultivating the wish to repay their kindness (*drin gzo*), developing the affection which sees them as lovable (*yid 'ong byams pa*), cultivating compassion (*snying rje*), the special wish (*lhag bsam*) and the actual altruistic intention (*sems bskyed*). The basis for these steps is boundless equanimity (*tshad med btang snyom*).

5. Equalizing and exchanging self and others (*bdag gzhan mnyam brje*) initially involves training ourselves to cherish others as much as we cherish ourselves (*bdag gzhan mnyam pa*), in that we are as much concerned about their happiness and suffering as we are about our own. We then continue by examining the faults of

selfishness from many points of view (*rang gces 'dzin gyi skyon sgo du ma nas bsam pa*) and the numerous advantages of cherishing others (*gzhan gces 'dzin gyi yon tan sgo du ma nas bsam pa*) until we are able to switch our attitude entirely (*bdag gzhan brje ba'i bsam pa dngos*). Previously we have been totally concerned with ourselves and have neglected others. Now our concern will be entirely for their well-being and we will forget about ourselves. To strengthen love which wishes to give others happiness and compassion which wishes to alleviate their suffering we do the practice of taking and giving (*gtong len*).

6. These lines are from Ashvaghosha's *Hundred and Fifty Verse Praise* (*Śatapañcāśatkastotra, brGya lnga cu pa'i stod pa*, P2038, Vol. 46).

7. Chandrakirti's *Supplement to the Middle Way* (*Madhyamakāvatāra, dBu ma la 'jug pa*, P5261, P5262, Vol. 98) is a commentary on Nagarjuna's *Treatise on the Middle Way* (*Madhyamakaśāstra, dBu ma'i bstan bcos*, P5224, Vol. 95), also called *Fundamental Wisdom* (*rTsa shes*), which it supplements by way of the extensive aspect of the path, the practice of skillful means. The subject-matter of *The Supplement* is presented in terms of the ten Bodhisattva stages. For a translation of the first five chapters, see Jeffrey Hopkins, *Compassion in Tibetan Buddhism* (London: Rider, 1980; rpt. Ithaca: Snow Lion, 1985) and for the translation of the sixth chapter, see Anne Klein, *Path to the Middle* (Albany: State University of New York Press, 1994).

8. *Sāgaramatiparipṛcchāsūtra, Blo gros rgya mtshos zhus pa'i mdo*, P819, Vol. 33.

9. The three realms are the desire, form and formless realms (*'dod khams, gzugs khams, gzugs med khams*). The desire realm includes hell-beings, hungry spirits, animals, humans, demi-gods and celestial beings belonging to this realm. There are seventeen abodes within the form realm, rebirth in which results from the practice of meditative stabilization. There are four abodes within the formless realm in which one is born as a result of more subtle states of meditative stabilization and through viewing the form realm as a coarse state and the formless realm as refined and preferable. All these states of rebirth are still within cyclic existence. The three realms sometimes also refer to what is below, on and above the ground.

10. In 1921 the eminent Gelugpa master Pabongka Rinpoche (Pha bong kha rin po che, also known to his disciples as Bla ma bDe

chen snying po, 1878-1941) gave a discourse on the stages of the path to enlightenment to a gathering of seven hundred monks, nuns and lay people near Lhasa. Kyabje Trijang Rinpoche (sKyabs rje Khri byang rin po che Blo bzang ye shes, 1901-1981), a close disciple of Pabongka Rinpoche, was present and made a transcript of each day's teaching. He later compiled and edited these transcripts which were published as *Liberation in the Palm of Your Hand* (rNam sgrol lag bcangs), containing the practical inspiring advice and vivid anecdotes characteristic of an oral teaching. Kyabje Trijang Rinpoche belonged to the monastic university of Ganden and was Junior Tutor to His Holiness the Dalai Lama. He was one of the outstanding scholars of his time. For an English translation of this work, see Michael Richard's *Liberation in the Palm of Your Hand* (Boston: Wisdom Publications, 1991).

11. After fleeing Tibet as a result of the Chinese invasion, a large number of monks lived in what had formerly been a British internment camp in Buxaduar. They were already in poor health after the difficult and dangerous journey they had made across the Himalayas. Some, like the Venerable Geshe Sonam Rinchen, entered India via the jungles of Assam. The living conditions in which they now found themselves were extremely spartan and many monks died from sickness, being unaccustomed to the heat and humidity and to the food, which apart from being very different from their normal diet was totally inadequate. The Venerable Geshe Sonam Rinchen also fell ill and spent a month in a hospital in Cooch Behar, where there was no one who spoke even one word of Tibetan. Two Indian nurses took pity on him and looked after him very kindly. While he was in hospital he completed a short retreat, reciting the mantra in praise of Je Tsongkhapa a hundred thousand times. He tells that his stomach problems were eventually cured after he performed a hundred thousand prostrations in Bodhgaya.

12. Dharmakirti of Suvarnadvipa (gSer gling pa Chos kyi grags pa) was a member of the ruling family during the Shailendra Empire. He is known as the master of "the Golden Isles." This term was used to refer to Sumatra, Java and the islands of the eastern archipelago. The empire also included a large part of the Malay archipelago and Malay peninsula. In the Tengyur (bsTan 'gyur) there are six works attributed to him, of which one states that it was written in Vijayanagara of Suvarnadvipa. This was the old port and

capital of Sumatra. Of these six works, five were translated into Tibetan with Atisha's participation. One of them is an extremely long commentary on the Perfection of Wisdom sutras which indicates the master's command of Mahayana philosophy. He enjoyed considerable stature as a teacher and exponent of Buddhism and had other Indian students besides Atisha. He certainly visited India and may have spent some time studying at Vikramashila, where Atisha later lived before he traveled to Tibet.

13. In his *Great Exposition of the Stages of the Path* Je Tsongkhapa mentions this sutra as *Bu mo zla ba mchog gis zhus pa*, which is listed in the Tibetan Tripitaka as *Candrottarādārikāvyākaraṇasūtra, Bu mo zla ba mchog lung bstan pa'i mdo*, P858, Vol. 34.

14. Kamalashila's *Stages of Meditation* (*Bhāvanākrama, sGom pa'i rim pa*, P5310-12, Vol. 102) has three parts. The first explains primarily how selflessness is established through hearing and thinking. The second part describes how to meditate on selflessness and the third delineates the results of doing this. Each part stands as a complete work in itself.

Chapter 3: Cultivating Loving Affection

1. Self-interest (*rang don gyi blo*) includes everything from the crassest selfishness to the wish for personal liberation from cyclic existence. Interest in the well-being of others (*gzhan don gyi blo*) extends from concern for their ordinary everyday needs to the wish for their highest enlightenment.

2. The four kinds of conditions which give rise to a moment of consciousness are the focal condition (*dmigs rkyen*), the main condition (*bdag rkyen*), the immediately preceding condition (*de ma thag rkyen*) and the causal conditions (*rgyu rkyen*), which include the above-mentioned three conditions as well as all other contributing factors. Taking as an example a moment of visual consciousness, its focal condition or object is a visible form. The main condition is the eye sense faculty, and the immediately preceding condition is a moment of consciousness which occurs immediately before the arising of the visual consciousness. The causal conditions include all of these and such factors as the potential for eye consciousness to arise and the eye itself, the seat of the sense faculty.

3. This image of the Buddha (referred to as the *rJo bo,* or Lord) was considered the most precious image in the whole of Tibet. It is said to have been made during the Buddha's lifetime. From India it was taken to China, and later, in the middle of the seventh century, brought to Tibet by King Srongtsen Gampo's (Srong brtsan sgam po) Chinese wife. Srongtsen Gampo was responsible for firmly establishing Buddhism in Tibet. Ordained and lay people throughout Tibet aspired to make a pilgrimage to see this image. To do so was considered to be as good as seeing the Buddha himself and receiving his blessings.

4. The proponents of the four schools of Buddhist philosophical tenets are the Vaibhashikas (Bye brag smra ba), the Sautrantikas (mDo sde pa), the Chittamatrins (Sems tsam pa) and the Madhyamikas (dBu ma pa), consisting of the Svatantrikas (Rang rgyud pa) and the Prasangikas (Thal 'gyur pa). See Sopa and Hopkins, *Cutting Through Appearances: Practice and Theory of Tibetan Buddhism* (Ithaca: Snow Lion Publications, 1989), for a succinct presentation of these systems of thought.

5. One section of the Chittamatrin school, who were mainly followers of Asanga and are known as the followers of scripture, posit eight kinds of consciousness: the five kinds of sense consciousness (*dbang shes*), mental consciousness (*yid shes*), foundational consciousness (*kun gzhi*) and afflicted mind (*nyon yid*). Afflicted mind mainly consists of misconceptions of the self. Foundational consciousness, which is unobstructed and neutral, carries the imprints of past virtuous and non-virtuous actions.

6. The developmental disposition: *rgyes 'gyur gyi rigs.* The naturally abiding or innate disposition: *rang bzhin gnas rigs.*

7. Shantideva's *Compendium of Training* (*Śikṣāsamuccaya, bsLabs pa kun las btus pa,* P5272, Vol. 102) is a compilation and elucidation of sutra passages related to the training of Bodhisattvas. English translation: Cecil Bendall and W.H.D. Rouse, *Śikṣa Samuccaya* (London: 1922; rpt. Delhi: Motilal Banarsidass, 1971).

8. Chandragomin's *Letter to a Disciple* (*Śiṣyalekha, Slob springs,* P5683, Vol. 129) was addressed to a monk who wished to enter into a relationship with a princess. In this letter of advice Chandragomin reminds him of the reasons for safeguarding his precepts

of training, the benefits derived from this and the disadvantages of not doing so.

9. *Heart of the Middle Way* (*Madhyamakahṛdaya, dBu ma'i snying po,* P5255, Vol. 96) by Bhavaviveka (Legs ldan 'byed, c. 500-570?). The main subject-matter of the text is how to accomplish one's own and others' good by means of three kinds of conduct: how never to be separated from the altruistic intention; how to cultivate the discipline of Bodhisattvas; and how to prevent the mind from holding extreme views through making effort in understanding suchness in a way that does not conflict with scriptural passages and reasoning.

CHAPTER 4: LOVE AND COMPASSION

1. These lines are found in Je Tsongkhapa's praise to the Buddha entitled *Those of the Three Times* (*sKabs gsum pa*). *sKabs gsum pa* is the name given to the celestial beings who are aware of three points in time: the previous rebirth from which they have come, the rebirth they are in and the rebirth to which they will go. The title is taken from the first words of the praise, in which the Buddha is extolled as the lord of all celestial beings.

2. Atisha is said to have studied with Shila Dharmarakshita at the monastic university of Odantapuri. Dharmarakshita is now best known for his work *The Wheel of Sharp Weapons (Blo byong mtshon cha 'khor lo)*, a text in the mind training tradition which explains how the many difficulties and troubles we experience are the result of our own past negative actions. His verses evoke particular situations and the specific actions responsible for producing them, demonstrating how the wheel of sharp weapons returns full circle upon us for wrongs we have done. English translation of the text and commentary by Geshe Ngawang Dhargye, Sharpa Tulku, Khamlung Tulku, Alexander Berzin and Jonathan Landaw (Dharamsala: LTWA, 1981).

3. Chenrezig (sPyan ras gzigs, Avalokiteśvara in Sanskrit) embodies enlightened compassion. Iconographically Chenrezig is most often depicted in a four-armed and in a thousand-armed form. The latter has eleven heads: the top head is the red face of Amitabha Buddha in an emanation body form with a crown protrusion and

212 The Bodhisattva Vow

no jewels. Below this is a fierce black face with fangs, glaring eyes and flaming tresses. Below this are three heads; the central one is red, that to its left is white and that to its right is green. Below these are three more heads which are, in the same order, green, red and white respectively. Below these are three more: white, green and red respectively. These nine heads all have peaceful eyes.

The first two hands touch at the heart with a hollow between them symbolizing the form and wisdom bodies of enlightened beings. The second right hand holds crystal prayer beads, representing skillful means. The third right hand is in the gesture of supreme giving. From it flows nectar alleviating the hunger and thirst of hungry ghosts. This gesture denotes the promise to bestow everything that is needed, and the common as well as powerful attainments. The fourth right hand holds a wheel which denotes the uninterrupted turning of the wheel of teaching for living beings.

The second left hand holds an unsullied lotus to show that Chenrezig is untainted by any trace of selfishness. It also represents wisdom. The third left hand holds a water pot to symbolize the washing away of all disturbing attitudes and emotions. The fourth holds a bow and arrow to show that by teaching living beings he will lead them to the path that combines skillful means and wisdom. The other nine hundred and ninety-two arms and hands symbolize his ability to emanate universal monarchs. The eyes in the palms of the hands represent the ability to emanate the thousand Buddhas of the fortunate era. All this is for the benefit of living beings.

4. Nagarjuna's Six Collections of Reasoning consist of the following: *Precious Garland of Advice for the King* (*Rājaparikathāratnāvalī*, rGyal po la gtam bya ba rin po che'i phreng ba, P5658, Vol. 129), *Refutation of Objections* (*Vigrahavyāvartanı*, rTsod pa bzlog pa, P5228, Vol. 95), *Seventy Stanzas on Emptiness* (*Śūnyatāsaptati*, sTong pa nyid bdun cu pa, P5227, Vol. 95), *Sixty Stanzas of Reasoning* (*Yuktiṣaṣṭika*, Rigs pa drug cu pa, P5225, Vol. 95), *Treatise Called "Finely Woven"* (*Vaidalyasūtra*, Zhib mo rnam par 'thag pa'i mdo, P5226, Vol. 95), *Treatise on the Middle Way* (*Madhyamakaśāstra*, dBu ma'i bstan bcos, also referred to as rTa ba shes rab in Tibetan, P5224, Vol. 95).

5. The "Practitioner of Love" (Byams pa'i rnal 'byor pa) possibly refers to Maitripa, also known as Maitrinatha, who was born at the beginning of the eleventh century and died at the age of seventy-eight.

6. Geshe Chekawa (dGe bshes mChad kha ba, 1101-1175), the author of the *Seven Points for Training the Mind* (*Blo sbyong don bdun ma*), was inspired by Geshe Langritangpa's (dGe bshes Glang ri thang pa, 1054-1123) words from the *Eight Verses for Training the Mind* (*Blo sbyong tshig brgyad ma*), "May I accept the loss and offer the victory to others." Geshe Chekawa traveled to central Tibet in search of their author to learn more about this practice. To his sorrow Geshe Langritangpa had already passed away, but he was able to receive teaching from Geshe Sharawa (dGe bshes Sha ra ba, 1070-1141), who also held the instructions.

7. Kyabje Trijang Rinpoche's commentary on Geshe Chekawa's *Seven Points for Training the Mind* is called *Blo sbyong don bdun ma'i rtsa gzhung gi mchan 'grel*.

CHAPTER 5: TRANSFORMING ATTITUDES

1. *Nagas* (*klu*) are said to be serpentine creatures, belonging to the realm of animals, who live in water. Some have a jewel on the crown of their heads. The more important *nagas* live in seas and oceans and own palaces and fabulous wealth. Lesser *nagas* live in springs and lakes. If one's conduct pleases them, they send or stop rain, whichever is needed. They like cleanliness and if one pollutes their dwelling places, they take offense and may cause skin and other diseases. The Mahayana teachings were given into their safekeeping.

2. Geshe Bengungyel ('Ban gung rgyal), one of the Kadampa masters, had been a thief and brigand earlier in his life. Later, after he had reformed, he used to chide himself when he noticed that he was doing or thinking anything unwholesome. He would say, "There you go again, you villain Bengungyel, still at your old ways!" But when he had done or thought something good, he would use his religious name and say, "Congratulations, Geshe Tsultrim Gyelwa, keep up the good work!"

3. The Indian master known as Padampa or Dampa Sangye (Dam pa sangs rgyas, d. 1117) in Tibet was a contemporary of the great practitioner Milarepa (Mi la ras pa, 1040-1123) and a teacher of Machig Labdron (Ma gcig lab sgron, 1055-1153), who is regarded as the mother of the practice of "cutting through" (*gcod*) in Tibet.

4. The eight worldly concerns (*'jig rten chos brgyad*) are being pleased when we receive gifts, when things go well, when we hear what is

agreeable and when we are praised, and being displeased when we don't receive gifts, when things go badly, when we hear what is disagreeable and when we are criticized. These concerns keep us preoccupied with the well-being of this life and prevent us from focusing on well-being in future lives.

5. Geshe Potowa (Po to ba Rin chen gsal, 1031-1105) entered Reting Monastery (Rwa sgreng) in 1058 and later became its abbot for a short time. He was mainly active in Penyul ('Phan yul) and is said to have had two thousand disciples. Today his best known work is the *Precious Heap of Analogies for the Teachings (dPe chos rin chen spungs pa)*, an anthology of analogies and stories illustrating many points of the Buddha's teachings. He put this volume together because he suspected that those he was teaching at times found it difficult to understand the teachings. He used analogies he had heard from his own spiritual teachers, stories that he found in the sutras and whatever he heard that was striking and relevant.

6. The six preliminary practices (*sbyor ba'i chos drug*) are (1) to clean the surroundings and room where one intends to practice (*gnas khang byi dor bya ba*) and to set up representations of enlightened body, speech and mind (*sku gsung thugs kyi rten bkram pa*); (2) to find offerings that are free from deceit (*mchod pa g.yo med par btsal ba*) and to arrange them beautifully (*bkod pa mdzes par bshams pa*); (3) to sit on a comfortable seat in the eight-point position (of Vairochana) or in some other comfortable position (*stan bde ba la lus 'dug lugs brgyad dam spyod lam gang bder 'khod pa*) and then in an especially virtuous state of mind to take refuge and arouse the altruistic intention (*dge sems khyad par can gyi ngang nas skyabs 'gro sems bskyed bya ba*); (4) visualize the field of accumulation (*tshogs zhing gsal 'debs pa*); (5) perform the seven-part practice which includes the essentials for purification and the accumulation of merit (*bsags sbyang gi gnad bsdus pa yan lag bdun pa bya ba*) and offer the mandala; (6) make requests and definitely mingle your mind (with the object of meditation) according to the instructions (*gsol ba 'debs pa man ngag bzhin rgyud dang 'dres nges su bya ba*).

The position of Vairochana has seven physical features. (1) The legs are placed in the vajra position, which creates an auspicious precedent for attaining the vajra position of the energy channels, winds and constituents during the stage of completion in the practice of tantra. Although this position is initially not easy to hold, it can be maintained for long periods when one is accustomed to it.

Keeping the lower part of the body locked in this way prevents ailments caused by cold, but the upper part of the body should be as relaxed as possible to prevent disturbances of the energy winds. (2) The hands are in the position of meditative equipoise four finger-widths below the navel, with the back of the right hand resting on the palm of the left. The thumbs touch, thereby creating a triangle. This position of the hands symbolizes activation of the psychic heat centered at the navel. (3) The elbows are kept away from the body to allow a flow of air under the arms which prevents slackness and lethargy in meditation. (4) The spine is kept straight to bring the energy channels into the best position for free movement of the energy winds. (5) The chin is slightly tucked in to inhibit the upward-flowing energy winds, which cause agitation when uncontrolled. (6) The mouth is neither open nor tightly closed, but relaxed with the tip of the tongue touching the upper palate behind the front teeth. This prevents thirst and drooling during long periods of meditative absorption. (7) The eyes are neither wide open, which encourages distraction, nor tightly closed, which can lead to sleepiness. They are loosely focused in line with the tip of one's nose. The eighth feature associated with the position of Vairochana is to focus on the breath, following one's inhalation and exhalation for some time in order to calm the mind.

7. In relation to the field of accumulation (*tshogs zhing*) practitioners accumulate merit through making prostrations, offerings, requests and so forth.

8. There are many versions of this seven-part practice (*yan lag bdun pa*). The words are intended to help the practitioner perform the seven activities which create positive energy and purify wrongdoing, the necessary basis for all other practices. Homage or obeisance (*phyag 'tshal ba*) is made to Buddhas, Bodhisattvas and all noble beings who are our inspiration. We then make actual and imagined gifts to them (*mchod pa phul ba*), acknowledge our wrongdoing (*bshags pa phul ba*), rejoice (*rjes su yi rang ba*) in our own and others' virtue, request (*bskul ba*) the enlightened ones to teach in order to dispel the darkness of ignorance, supplicate (*gsol ba 'debs pa*) them not to pass away but to remain in the world to which they bring light, and dedicate (*bsngo ba*) our merit in general and specifically that which is created through the performance of this practice to the peace, happiness and complete enlightenment of all living beings.

9. In this context a mandala is a representation of the universe and everything precious within it offered as a gift to all those in whom one takes refuge, such as one's spiritual teachers, meditational deities, Buddhas and Bodhisattvas. The representation may be created on a round base, commonly made of copper or silver, on which heaps of rice or grain, which may be colored with a natural dye, are placed within three rings, stacked one on top of the other. As each handful of rice representing different elements of the universe is added, the appropriate words are recited. Shells, beads and semiprecious or precious stones are often mixed with the rice. However, if one does not possess such things, very simple materials may also be used, since offering the mandala is primarily an act of imagination. The universe can also be represented by a hand gesture which is made while reciting the verses. In certain practices one imagines the various parts of one's body becoming the different elements which make up the universe to be offered.

10. In his *Precious Garland* Nagarjuna says, "May their wrong-doing ripen on me and may my virtue ripen on them." In his *Way of the Bodhisattva* Shantideva says, "The pains and sorrows of all wandering beings—may they ripen wholly on myself." The tenth chapter of Shantideva's work offers us many inspiring verses of aspiration.

11. The seven-part cause and effect process and the instructions for equalizing self and others may be combined in different ways. The following is a combination consisting of thirteen steps: (1) cultivating equanimity, (2) recognizing all beings as our mothers, (3) remembering their kindness, (4) wanting to repay their kindness, (5) equalizing self and others, (6) considering the faults of selfishness from many points of view, (7) considering the benefits of cherishing others from many points of view, (8) why it is appropriate to cherish others, (9) actual exchange of self and others, (10) giving to strengthen love, (11) taking to strengthen compassion, (12) the special wish and (13) the altruistic intention.

CHAPTER 6: HOW TO HOLD THE ALTRUISTIC INTENTION

1. A stupa (*mchod rten*) is a reliquary and usually contains relics of a great practitioner, texts and other sacred objects. Small portable stupas may be made of silver or gold and studded with precious

stones. There are eight different kinds of stupas with variations in the architectural features. The various parts of a stupa represent the different powers and abilities of an enlightened being's mind. On a shrine the stupa is set to the left of an image of the Buddha, which represents the body of an enlightened being, while a text is placed to the right of the image and represents enlightened speech. Stupas may also be made of masonry and may be tall buildings such as the main stupa in Bodhgaya, which marks the place where the Buddha Shakyamuni attained enlightenment. Everyday implements and tools of different kinds are often placed within the base of larger stupas. These represent all the things necessary for daily life and are included to bring auspiciousness and prosperity to the area in which the stupa is being constructed.

2. Samye Monastery (bSam yas mi 'gyur lhun gyi grub pa'i gtsug lag khang), the first monastery in Tibet, was built during the reign of Trisong Detsen (Khri srong lde btsan, eighth century). The first seven Tibetans monks were ordained there. It is said to have been modeled on an Indian monastery called Ogyenpuri (O rgyan pu ri), probably Odantapuri, and that while Samye was under construction, the work done by the builders during the day was destroyed by hostile spirits at night. This continued until Padmasambhava blessed the monastery, after which the spirits became so cooperative that they carried on building during the night. The bottom storey was constructed of stone in the Tibetan style. The middle storey was built of bricks in the Chinese style and the top storey was made of wood in the Indian style. Many earlier translations were revised at Samye, whose library contained many precious treasures. The contents of this library were dispersed during the Cultural Revolution, when many volumes were taken to Beijing.

3. The *Essence of Refined Gold* (*Byang chub lam gyi rim pa'i khrid yig gser zhun ma*) is a text on the stages of the path to enlightenment written by the third Dalai Lama, Sonam Gyatso (bSod nams rgya mtsho, 1543-1588). English translation: Glenn H. Mullin, *Selected Works of the Dalai Lama III, Essence of Refined Gold* (Ithaca: Snow Lion Publications, 1982); reprinted as *The Path to Enlightenment* by H. H. the Dalai Lama (Ithaca: Snow Lion Publications, 1995).

4. Construction of Norbulingka (Nor bu gling kha), the summer residence of the Dalai Lamas just outside the periphery of Lhasa proper, which is marked by the outer circumambulation route (*gling*

'khor), began during the reign of the seventh Dalai Lama, Kelsang Gyatso (bsKal bzang rgya mtsho, 1708-1757) with the building of the first palace, called bsKal bzang pho brang. Successive Dalai Lamas built residences on this site which eventually formed a complex of beautiful palaces. The surrounding area was a favorite place for picnics.

5. Ganden Monastery (dGa' ldan) was founded in 1409, Drepung ('Bras spung) in 1416 and Sera Monastery (Se ra) in 1419. These were the principal Gelugpa monastic universities in Tibet.

6. These Bodhisattvas are called "irreversible" *(phyir mi ldog pa'i byang chub sems dpa')* because they will never forsake their commitment to attain enlightenment for the good of all living beings. Those with the sharpest faculties display forty-six physical and verbal signs that allow one to infer their inner realizations on the path of preparation. Those with intermediate faculties do so on the path of seeing, while those with the dullest faculties do so on the eighth Bodhisattva stage.

7. Taking refuge in the teachings entails taking refuge in the third and fourth noble truths, namely in true cessation of suffering and in the paths which lead to that state. The teachings have two aspects: the scriptural teachings *(lung gi bstan pa)* and realization of the teachings *(rtogs pa'i bstan pa).* The former refers to the teachings themselves and the latter is any aspect of the excellent teachings, based on taking refuge, which belongs to the three kinds of training—in ethical discipline, concentration or wisdom. In other words it refers to the embodiment of the teachings in the form of realizations one has gained or hopes to gain through practice.

8. Those who have made a formal commitment to take refuge in the Three Jewels observe certain precepts. The individual precepts concern what should and should not be done with regard to each of the Three Jewels. The precepts in relation to the Buddha are that one should not consider any other refuge or source of protection higher than the Buddha and should respect all images of the Buddha and enlightened beings, whether or not they are well made or made of something precious.

The precepts in relation to the teachings are, as far as possible, not to harm other living beings and to respect all texts which contain instruction on what behavior and attitudes to adopt and what to discard, since they are intended for one's own and others' well-being.

The precepts in relation to the spiritual community are not to allow one's physical, verbal or mental activity to be influenced by those who dislike and oppose the Buddha's teaching and to respect all members of the spiritual community, no matter which form of Buddhism they practice, regarding them as spiritual companions, offering them material help and fostering a relationship with them based on the teachings.

The general precepts are to take refuge again and again, remembering the special qualities and distinguishing features of the Three Jewels; to offer the first and best part of food and drink and to make other offerings, remembering the kindness of the Three Jewels; to encourage others who show an interest to take refuge; to entrust oneself to the Three Jewels in whatever activities one undertakes; not to give up the Three Jewels even in joke or at the cost of one's life; to take refuge three times each day and three times each night, remembering the benefits of doing so: (1) one becomes a Buddhist (2) and a suitable basis for all vows; (3) formerly accumulated karmic obstructions come to an end; (4) extensive stores of positive energy are easily accumulated; (5) harm from humans and non-humans cannot affect one; (6) one will not take bad rebirths; (7) one will accomplish all one's wishes; (8) one will become enlightened quickly.

9. The *King of Prayers*, also known as the *Prayer of Noble Conduct* (*Samantabhadracaryāpraṇidhānarāja, Kun tu bzang po spyod pa'i smon lam gyi rgyal po*), is part of the *Avatamsaka Sutra*. It summarizes the deeds of Bodhisattvas described at length in this sutra. The *King of Prayers* is also found in the tantra (*rgyud*) section of the Buddha's teachings (P716, Vol. 11).

10. *Lam rim bsdus don / Byang chub lam gyi rim pa'i nyams len gyi rnam gzhag mdor bsdus*, The Collected Works of Rje Tsoṅ-kha-pa Blo-bzaṅ-grags-pa, Vol. kha, *thor bu*, 65b.2-68b.1 (New Delhi: Ngawang Gelek Demo, 1975). For an English translation of the verses by Ruth Sonam, see "The Abridged Stages of the Path to Enlightenment" in *Chö Yang* No. 7 (Sidhpur: Norbulingka Institute, 1996).

11. The four ways of maturing others (*bsdu ba'i dngos po bzhi*) are skillful means employed to gain others' trust and make them mentally

mature and receptive to increasingly profound teachings. Since most ordinary people are attracted by material generosity, Bodhisattvas first give gifts (*sbyin pa*) and act generously towards those they intend to help in order to establish a positive relationship. When a suitable opportunity arises they teach in an informal, interesting and pleasant way adapted to the other person's capacities and inclinations (*snyan par smra ba*). They then encourage him or her to apply in practice what was explained (*don spyod pa*). At the same time, they take care to validate the advice they have given through personal example (*don mthun pa*).

12. Tara (sGrol ma), the embodiment of enlightened activity and the manifestation of purified energy, is mainly represented in her green and white forms. Green Tara sits with her right leg extended as though ready to rise and help those in need. Her left hand is at her heart, and between the ring finger and thumb, which represent the joining of skillful means and wisdom, she holds the stem of a blue *utpala* flower. The other three fingers are raised to denote the Three Jewels. With her right hand she makes the gesture of supreme giving by which she promises to give everything we desire—both temporary and ultimate happiness. The expression on her face is a little fierce and her vigilant eyes are wide open. She is full of energy since she embodies the swift action of enlightened beings. Her green color is associated with the wisdom which accomplishes things.

White Tara sits in the lotus position making the same gesture with her hands. She has five extra eyes: one on the sole of each foot and on the palm of each hand as well as one in the middle of her forehead. She is associated with longevity and with the pacification of disease and obstacles.

The Kadampa masters liked to depict Tara with two companions. The Frowning One (Khro gnyer can ma) on the left of Tara is black. She is adorned with jewels, sits in the half vajra position and holds a curved knife and skullcup. On the right of Tara is the Radiant One ('Od zer can ma), who is yellow in color, adorned with jewels, sits in the half vajra position and holds a branch of the Ashoka tree in her right hand and a flower in her left hand.

13. Deceit: *g.yo*; pretense: *sgyu*.

14. The *Cloud of Jewels Sutra, Ratnameghasūtra, dKon mchog sprin gyi mdo*, P879, Vol. 35.

15. The *Sutra with Three Parts,* also called the *Confession Sutra, Triskandhakasūtra, Phung bo gsum pa'i mdo,* P950, Vol. 37.

CHAPTER 7: THE ETHICAL DISCIPLINE OF BODHISATTVAS

1. The Mahayana or Great Vehicle (*theg pa chen po*) consists of the causal Perfection Vehicle (*rgyu pha rol tu chin pa'i theg pa*) and the resultant Secret Mantra Vehicle (*'bras bu gsang sngags kyi theg pa*). The Perfection Vehicle is the body of practices described in the Mahayana sutras by which a Bodhisattva creates the great stores of merit and insight necessary for enlightenment over three incalculably long aeons. The Secret Mantra Vehicle is the body of practices described in the tantras through which enlightenment can be attained in one short lifetime. These practices are suitable for practitioners of the very highest caliber. By virtue of simulating the desired result, enlightenment, through tantric practice, the result actually comes into being.

2. Asanga's *Bodhisattva Stages* (*Yogacaryābhūmaubodhisattvabhūmi, rNal 'byor spyod pa'i sa las byang chub sems dpa'i sa,* P5538, Vol. 110) explains the paths of the Great Vehicle while its companion volume, the *Hearer Stages* (*Śrāvakabhūmi, Nyan sa,* P5537, Vol. 110), explains the paths of practice of the Lesser Vehicle.

3. One of these is Sakya Pandita Kunga Gyeltsen's (Sa skya pandita Kun dga' rgyal mtshan, 1182-1251) *Analysis of the Three Vows* (*sDom pa gsum gyi rab tu dbye pa'i bstan bcos*). Another is the *String of Brilliant Jewels: Instructions on the Individual Liberation, the Bodhisattva and the Tantric Vows* (*So thar byang sems gsang sngag gsum gyi sdom pa'i bslab bya nor bu'i 'od 'phreng*) by Tsenshap Tsewang Samdrup (mTshan zhabs Tshe dbang bsam 'grub), debating tutor to the tenth Dalai Lama, Tsultrim Gyatso (Tshul khrims rgya mtsho, 1816-1837). Also see *Buddhist Ethics,* translated into English and edited by the International Translation Committee founded by the V.V. Kalu Rinpoche (Ithaca: Snow Lion Publications, 1998), which contains the fifth book of Jamgön Kongtrul Lodrö Tayé's (Kong sprul Blo gros mtha' yas, 1813-1899) *Infinite Ocean of Knowledge* (*Shes bya mtha' yas pa'i rgya mtsho*).

4. There are different versions of the *Six Session Guru Yoga* (*Thun drug bla ma'i rnal 'byor*). A long and a short version were written by Pabongka Rinpoche (Pha bong kha rin po che, Byams pa bstan 'dzin

'phrin las rgya mtsho, 1878-1941), the eminent Gelugpa master and the foremost spiritual teacher of His Holiness the fourteenth Dalai Lama's junior tutor, Kyabje Trijang Rinpoche. The long form of the *Six Session Guru Yoga* lists the primary transgressions of the Bodhisattva vow and of the tantric vow. By reciting the text we remind ourselves of these and of the various pledges associated with the practice of tantra. This allows us to ascertain whether any transgressions of these pledges have occurred, so that we can take steps to purify them. According to the *Indestructible Peak Tantra* (*Vajraśikharamahāguhyayogatantra, gSang ba rnal 'byor chen po'i rgyud rdo rje rtse mo*, P113, Vol. 5), certain pledges relating to the five Buddha families (*rgyal ba rigs lnga*) should be honored six times in twenty-four hours and failure to do so creates a serious fault. By performing the *Six Session Yoga* one keeps these pledges. This is an important aspect of how Bodhisattva conduct is practiced in the context of secret mantra.

5. *Twenty Verses on the Bodhisattva Vow* (*Bodhisattvasaṃvaraviṃśaka, Byang chub sems dpa'i sdom pa nyi shu pa*, P5582. Vol. 114) explains the eighteen main and forty-six secondary infractions of the Bodhisattva vow. See *Candragomin's Twenty Verses on the Bodhisattva Vow*, translated by Mark Tatz (Dharamsala: Library of Tibetan Works and Archives, 1982). This also contains a commentary, *Byang chub sems dpa'i sdom pa gsal bar ston pa shlo ka nyi shu pa'i rnam par bshad pa*, by Dragpa Gyaltsen (Grags pa rgyal mtshan, 1147-1216), one of the founders of the Sakya school.

6. The Tibetan term for ethical discipline is *tshul khrims*. By observing this code of conduct (*khrims*) we live in a way that accords with the actual condition (*gnas tshul*) of a true Bodhisattva.

7. There are eight kinds of individual liberation vow (*so sor thar pa'i sdom pa rigs brgyad*). The individual liberation vow (*so thar gyi sdom pa*) is so called because observing it enables an individual to attain liberation. It focuses primarily on the maintenance of pure physical and verbal conduct. Different forms of this vow are taken by lay and ordained people. The "vow of one who remains nearer" (*bsnyen gnas kyi sdom pa*), through which one draws closer to liberation, is taken for only twenty-four hours at a time and is therefore not considered equal to the others as a basis for the Bodhisattva

vow. It consists of restraint from (1) killing, (2) stealing, (3) lying and (4) sexual activity. One may not use (5) high or fancy seats, (6) intoxicants, (7) eat after midday, (8) wear garlands, jewelry or perfume, make music, dance or sing. This vow is taken by lay persons.

The second and third kinds of individual liberation vow, which are also taken by lay persons, are the "vow of one close to virtue" (*dge bsnyen gyi sdom pa*) for men and for women. Virtue here refers to nirvana. Both men and women vow to observe restraint from (1) killing, (2) stealing, (3) lying and (4) sexual misconduct. They also promise to refrain from the use of intoxicants.

The remaining kinds of individual liberation vow are taken by those who leave family life behind (*rab tu byung ba*). They must rely on an abbot, give up the signs of lay life, adopt the signs of ordained life and insure that they do not deviate from these three forms of conduct. The fourth and fifth kinds are "vows of those entering the path to virtue" (*dge tshul gyi sdom pa*), often referred to as novice monks' and nuns' vows. They involve restraint from (1) killing, (2) stealing, (3) lying and (4) sexual activity, from (5) making music, dancing or singing, (6) wearing garlands, jewelry or perfume, (7) accepting silver or gold with the intention of keeping them, (8) taking food after midday, (9) using ornate seats or (10) high seats.

The sixth is the "vow of a female trainee in virtue" (*dge slob ma'i sdom pa*). In preparation for becoming a fully ordained nun she must hold the vow of a novice nun and in addition practice restraint from twelve activities for two years. She must not (1) travel unless accompanied by someone who observes a similar code of discipline, (2) swim naked across a big river to reach the other side, (3) touch a man, (4) sit on the same seat as a man, (5) act as a matchmaker, (6) hide the transgressions of a female friend, (7) own gold or other valuables, (8) shave her pubic hair, (9) eat what has not been given to her, (10) eat food she has saved, (11) cut green grass and dispose of bodily excretions indiscriminately, or (12) dig the earth.

The seventh and eighth kinds are the "vows of those who strive for virtue" (*dge slong gi sdom pa* and *dge slong ma'i sdom pa*). A fully ordained nun must refrain from three hundred and sixty-four activities; a fully ordained monk from two hundred and fifty-three.

8. Those with the Bodhisattva vow exist in the lower realms and in the realms of celestial beings and humans. Celestial beings of the desire realm and humans can newly acquire the Bodhisattva vow, whereas those in the lower realms and in the form and formless realms can only hold the Bodhisattva vow which they received in a former lifetime and did not relinquish.

9. The ethical discipline of restraint from faulty action: *nye spyod sdom pa'i tshul khrims*; the ethical discipline of accumulating virtue: *dge ba'i chos sdud pa'i tshul khrims*; the ethical discipline of working for the good of sentient beings: *sems can don byed kyi tshul khrims*.

10. Individual liberation vows intended to curb the actions which result from the disturbing emotions: *nyon mongs rtse 'jil ba'i so thar gyi sdom pa*; the vow of concentration which temporarily prevents [the disturbing emotions from] arising even though the conditions [for this] are present: *rkyen yod kyang re zhig mi ldang ba'i bsam gtan gyi sdom pa*; the vow of non-contamination which severs the continuity [of the disturbing emotions]: *rgyun gcod pa'i zag med kyi sdom pa*.

11. The category of teachings that deals with the conduct of Bodhisattvas (*byang chub sems dpa'i sde snod*) in general refers to all literature explaining the practices of Bodhisattvas and in particular to the whole *Avatamsaka Sutra*, as mentioned earlier. The twelfth chapter of the *Heap of Jewels Sutra* (*Mahāratnakūṭasūtra, dKon mchog brtsegs pa'i mdo*, P760, Vols. 22-24) is entitled *Bodhisattvapiṭaka, Byang chub sems dpa'i sde snod*.

12. While all prayers of dedication (*sngo ba*) are prayers of aspiration (*smon lam*) the converse is not true. When making a dedication we need something to dedicate, such as the positive energy we have created by performing a certain practice or showing kindness to others. We dedicate this to act as a cause for others' temporary and ultimate well-being.

13. The *Sutra on the Ten Stages* (*Daśabhūmikasūtra, mDo sde sa bcu pa*, P761.31, Vol. 25) forms part of the *Avatamsaka Sutra*.

14. *Offerings to the Spiritual Teacher* (*Zab lam bla ma mchod pa'i cho ga*) was written by Penchen Losang Chökyi Gyeltsen (Pan chen Blo bzang chos kyi rgyal mtshan, 1569-1662). This text contains an inspiring prayer to make when practicing giving and taking:

And thus my holy compassionate teachers, bless me
So that all suffering, wrong-doing and obstructions
Of all motherly living beings ripen now on me.
And by sending them my happiness and virtue
May all living creatures be possessed of happiness.

15. Wölka ('Ol kha) is situated in the Loka (lHo kha) region of central Tibet.

16. The six different forms of super-knowledge or higher perception are as follows: knowledge of miraculous feats (*rdzu 'phrul gyi mngon shes*) allows Bodhisattvas to reach different worlds in order to find those with whom they have a particularly strong karmic connection. Through knowledge of others' minds (*gzhan sems shes pa'i mngon shes*) they are able to discern the different abilities, inclinations, interests and dispositions of those they wish to help, so that what they do will be entirely appropriate. With the divine ear (*lha'i rna ba'i mngon shes*), a form of clairaudience, they can hear what is going on in other worlds and pure lands. Knowledge of past places (*sngon gyi gnas rjes su dran pa'i mngon shes*) permits them to remember the spiritual teachers, people and practices with which they have had a close connection in the past. Clairvoyance, the divine eye (*lha'i mig gi mngon shes*), gives them the power to discern others' feelings of happiness or unhappiness. Knowing the end of contamination (*zag pa zad pa'i mngon shes*) is a personal understanding gained through meditation and higher perception of the paths of practice which lead to liberation, and of how to communicate this understanding to others.

17. The eleven ways in which Bodhisattvas work for the good of others is to act as a friend to those who need one (*grogs bya dgos pa*), to give advice to those who are confused (*thabs la rmongs pa*), to help those who need help (*phan 'dogs pa*), to protect those who are overwhelmed by fear (*'jigs pas nyen pa*), to comfort those who are tormented by grief (*mya ngan gyi gzir ba*), providing for those who lack things (*yo byad kyi phongs pa*), acting as a mentor to those who wish to meet a spiritual teacher (*gnas 'cha' bar 'dod pa*), and as a companion to those who seek someone like-minded (*blo mthun par 'dod pa*), praising those who are engaged in what is correct (*yang dag par zhugs pa*), admonishing those who are engaged in what is wrong (*log par zhugs pa*) and subduing those for whom it

is appropriate through magical feats (*rdzu 'phrul gyis gdul bar bya ba*).

CHAPTER 8: COMMENTARY ON CHANDRAGOMIN'S *TWENTY VERSES*

1. The word "transgressions" has been used to refer to both downfall (*ltung ba*) and faulty actions (*nyes byas*). In the context of the individual liberation vow the word "defeat" has been used to translate *pham pa*.

2. It is customary to decorate the place where the vow is to be given with garlands of white flowers and other white adornments to symbolize purity of intention. When white flowers are not available, the seeds of the *Oroxylum indicum* are strung together. This tree grows in India and Nepal. Its long, hard, dark brown seed pods, looking like flattened horns, are about the length of an arrow and contain numerous small, flat, white seeds each with a small white wing which resembles tissue-paper. These seeds, referred to as *me tog tsam pa ka*, were much prized in Tibet. In the Tibetan medical system a medicine to calm fevers is prepared from them.

They are also used as an offering to the deity when empowerments are conferred. One drops a single "flower" onto the mandala and the direction in which it falls determines the family of enlightened beings with whom one has a particular connection. The heads of the five families of Victorious Ones (*rgyal ba rigs lnga*) are Vairochana (rNam par snang mdzad), Ratnasambhava (Rin chen 'byung gnas), Amitabha ('Od dpag med), Amoghasiddhi (Don yod grub pa) and Akshobhya (Mi bskyod pa). They embody the purified aggregates of form, feeling, recognition, compositional factors and consciousness respectively.

3. Non-abiding nirvana (*mi gnas pa'i myang 'das*) refers to the highest state of enlightenment in which one is free from the fears associated with both worldly existence and solitary peace (*srid zhi 'jigs pa las grol ba*). Worldly existence is compared to a sea of poison and solitary peace is compared to an ocean of milk.

4. Instead of "because it is definite" (*nges pa'i phyir*) some versions of the text have *dge ba'i phyir*, which can be taken to mean "for the sake of virtue." According to this interpretation Buddhas and Bodhisattvas

rejoice in what the new Bodhisattva has done and in order to insure that his or her virtue will increase, they pray that it will always grow and never decline. It can also be taken to mean "there is virtue because." For that new Bodhisattva there is virtue because Buddhas and Bodhisattvas focus on him or her and pray that unhindered by obstacles his or her virtue will continually grow. This causes the Bodhisattva's virtue to increase.

5. The five kinds of transgressions with regard to the individual liberation vow of the ordained are called downfalls constituting the set of defeats (*ltung ba pham pa'i sde*) of which there are four; the set of remaining downfalls (*ltung ba lhag ma'i sde*) of which there are thirteen; the set which cause one to fall (*ltung byed kyi sde*) of which there are a hundred and twenty; the set which must be confessed individually (*sor bshags kyi sde*) of which there are four; and the set of faulty actions (*nyes byas kyi sde*) of which there are a hundred and twelve.

The set of defeats are so called because virtue is defeated by these actions and non-virtue triumphs. The vow that was taken becomes useless through these transgressions and is compared to the wealth of someone who owes an enormous debt. A person who left lay life behind and took the vow of a fully ordained monk becomes like a householder again. Such a person may no longer use what is offered to the community of the ordained, may not participate in rituals performed by the community nor live within it. Once such a basic defeat has been created there is no possibility of restoring the vow.

When a transgression belonging to the set of remaining downfalls is created, the vow can be restored with the spiritual community's consent. The community may impose a fine or a penalty consisting of work. An action belonging to the set which causes one to fall, if left unconfessed, makes one fall into a bad rebirth, in which one will be fettered or killed. The set which must be confessed individually should not be hidden but acknowledged aloud before the community with signs of regret and sorrow. The set of faulty actions contravenes both secular codes of conduct and those codes of conduct intended specifically for the ordained.

There are only two kinds of transgressions with regard to the Bodhisattva vow: basic downfalls (*rtsa ltung*) and faulty actions (*nyes byas*).

6. Although individual liberation vows may be held by both Mahayana and Hinayana practitioners, the main basis for the individual liberation vow is a practitioner of the Lesser Vehicle. Both those who are and who are not capable of attaining the state of Foe Destroyer in a particular lifetime put on the armor of wishing to extinguish all contamination and make effort as great as if their head or clothes were on fire. Only through such concerted effort is it possible to get rid of all contamination in the form of the disturbing emotions. The individual liberation vow is taken with such resolve.

There are two kinds of defeat with regard to the individual liberation vow: a defeat with the wish to hide what has been done and a defeat without such a wish. Anybody who creates a defeat with the wish to hide their action will not be able to bring contamination to an end in this life and so the main purpose for taking the individual liberation vow has been defeated. For practitioners of the Hearer Vehicle the individual liberation vow is the root of all virtue. When a defeat is created, there is a marked increase in shameless and indecent conduct, while one's sense of shame and decency decline. This precludes any possibility of taking the vow again.

When the Bodhisattva vow is lost, it can be taken again because its loss does not necessarily involve a lack of shame or embarrassment. Je Tsongkhapa, however, raises the point that one who has lost the individual liberation vow and then wishes to take the Bodhisattva vow may not actually be able to receive it because their sense of shame and embarrassment would have declined.

7. Great contamination: *zag pa chen po*; moderate contamination: *zag pa 'bring*; minor contamination: *zag pa chung ngu*.

8. The four binding factors (*kun dkris bzhi*) are not giving up the desire to act in a particular way and still wanting to do it (*spyod 'dod ma log pa dang da dung spyod 'dod pa*), taking joy and delight in it (*dga' zhing mgu ba*), lacking shame and embarrassment (*ngo tsha dang khrel med pa*) and not regarding the action as faulty (*nyes dmigs su mi lta ba*). The word "joy" (*dga'*) is explained as enjoyment of the action while one is doing it, and "delight" (*mgu*) as a whole-hearted liking for the action.

9. Reward: *rnyed pa*; respect and service: *bkur sti*.

10. Practices during the stage of completion (*rdzogs rim*) involve focusing intense attention on the energy channels, energy winds and

drops of the subtle body, particularly at the different centers, to generate great bliss. This blissful awareness is eventually used to apprehend emptiness and to produce the illusory body (*sgyu lus*).

11. In his commentary on Chandragomin's *Twenty Verses* (*Saṃvaraviṃśakavṛtti, sDom pa nyi shu pa'i 'grel ba*, P5583, Vol. 114) Shantarakshita (Zhi ba 'tsho, also known as mKhan chen bo dhi sa ttva, eighth century) says that any of the forty-six faulty actions should be confessed with remorse to someone suitable, but if such a person cannot be found, we should confess the transgression in our own mind with feelings of shame and embarrassment and with the determination not to perform the action again. Shantarakshita holds that the same applies to downfalls created with moderate or minor contamination.

In his commentary (*Bodhisattvasaṃvaraviṃśakapañjikā, Byang chub sems dpa'i sdom pa nyi shu pa'i dka' 'grel*, P5584, Vol. 114) Bodhibhadra (Byang chub bzang po, tenth century) emphasizes that the confession of downfalls performed with moderate and minor contamination is quite different from confession of the forty-six faulty actions. With regard to the former he says that if there is no one suitable to whom these transgressions can be confessed in the place where one lives, one must go to another place where such a person can be found. On the other hand, if it is not possible to find someone to whom any of the forty-six faulty actions can be confessed, one can confess them in one's own mind with a strong resolve not to repeat them.

In his *Highway to Enlightenment: An Explanation of Bodhisattva Discipline* (*Byang chub gzhung lam*, P6145, Vol. 154), which is a commentary on the chapter dealing with the discipline of Bodhisattvas in Asanga's *Bodhisattva Stages*, Je Tsongkhapa does not agree with Bodhibhadra but favors Shantarakshita's interpretation. Referring to Asanga's *Bodhisattva Stages* he says that where downfalls created with minor contamination and the forty-six faulty actions are concerned, if no one can be found to whom the action can be confessed, one should acknowledge it in one's mind with a strong resolve not to do it again and one will be absolved. Since this applies to downfalls created with minor contamination, he concludes that the same will apply to downfalls created with moderate contamination and that for purification a penalty need not necessarily be imposed. It is enough to have strong regret and the resolve not to repeat the action.

According to Tsenshap Tsewang Samdrup's *String of Brilliant Jewels* transgressions performed with moderate contamination should be confessed to three or more people, transgressions with minor contamination and any of the forty-six faulty actions should be confessed to at least one person and all other negativities to one person if one can. In case this is not possible, one should confess them in one's own mind imagining the presence of Buddhas and Bodhisattvas.

12. Certain commentators have said that the remaining transgressions can all be included within the four downfalls (consisting of eight actions) mentioned in Asanga's *Bodhisattva Stages* and in Chandragomin's *Twenty Verses*. Je Tsongkhapa states that this assertion is unreliable.

The transgressions enumerated by Shantideva in the *Compendium of Training* are those mentioned in the *Akashagarbha Sutra* (*Akāśagarbhasūtra, Nam mkha'i snying po'i mdo*, P926, Vol. 36), while those found in Chandragomin's *Twenty Verses*, which follows Asanga's *Bodhisattva Stages*, are not mentioned in *The Compendium*. The fact that neither *The Compendium* nor *Bodhisattva Stages* contains an exhaustive version of the transgressions does not present a problem, since both texts urge us to read the sutras dealing with Bodhisattva conduct in order to understand more fully the transgressions to be avoided.

It has been asserted that if one takes the Bodhisattva vow as described by Shantideva in the *Way of the Bodhisattva*, one need only refrain from the downfalls enumerated in *The Compendium* and that this is the Madhyamika way of taking the vow. If one follows Asanga's *Bodhisattva Stages*, which is the Cittamatrin way of taking the vow, one is committed to refrain from the transgressions listed in Asanga's text and in Chandragomin's *Twenty Verses*. This distinction based on philosophical tenets is, however, invalid.

13. Kyabje Yongdzin Ling Rinpoche (sKyabs rje Yongs 'dzin gLing rin po che, Thub bstan lung rtogs rnam rgyal 'phrin las, 1903-1984) was the senior tutor of His Holiness the fourteenth Dalai Lama. At the time of the Chinese invasion of Tibet the then Ganden Throne-holder (dGa' ldan khri pa) was unable to escape to India and until the former's death Kyabje Ling Rinpoche acted as his deputy. He then became Ganden Throne-holder himself and remained in this office until his death. He commanded great respect.

14. There were two tantric colleges in Lhasa: Gyutö (rGyud stod grwa tshang) and Gyumay (rGyud smad grwa tshang). These were the two principal Gelugpa centers for education relating to tantra. In exile both colleges continue their traditions with distinct styles of ritual and chanting. Gyumay has been reestablished at Hunsur in the Indian state of Karnataka, while Gyutö has been based near Bomdila in the Indian State of Arunachal Pradesh but will eventually move to a new monastery built near Dharamsala in Himachal Pradesh.

15. If effort to purify these five actions (*mtshams med lnga*) by applying the appropriate counteractions is not made, there will be no interval (*mtshams med pa*) between this life and one's immediate rebirth in a hell realm.

16. The Learners' Vehicle: *slob pa'i theg pa.*

17. The scriptural teachings (*lung gi bstan pa*) refer to the teachings of the Buddha himself and the commentaries on these teachings, all of which are subsumed under three categories (*sde snod gsum*): the teachings on discipline (*'dul ba'i sde snod*) mainly set forth the training in ethical discipline (*tshul khrims kyi bslab pa*) or conduct (*spyod pa*). The teachings contained in the compilation of sutras (*mdo sde'i sde snod*) principally explain the training in meditative stabilization (*ting nge 'dzin gyi bslab pa*) or meditation (*sgom pa*). The teachings on wisdom (*chos mngon pa'i sde snod*) primarily explain the training in wisdom (*shes rab kyi bslab pa*) or the view (*lta ba*). The realizations that are gained through practicing ethical discipline, meditative stabilization and wisdom constitute the insight aspect of the teachings (*rtogs pa'i bstan pa*).

18. "And for the sake of verses": *tshigs bcad rgyu yis.*

19. See the reference to the *Akashagarbha Sutra* in note 12 of this chapter.

20. Akashagarbha is one of the eight Bodhisattvas known as the eight close "sons" of the Buddha (*nye ba'i sras brgyad*). Though they have the same qualities and powers, each displays perfection in one particular area or activity: Manjushri ('Jam dpal dbyangs) embodies wisdom; Avalokiteshvara (sPyan ras gzigs) embodies compassion; Vajrapani (Phyag na rdo rje) embodies power; Kshitigarbha (Sa'i snying po) increases the richness and fertility of the land;

Sarvanirvarana Viskambhin (sGrib pa rnam sel) purifies wrong-doing and obstructions; Maitreya (Byams pa) embodies love; Samantabhadra (Kun tu bzang po) displays special expertise in making offerings and prayers of aspiration; Akashagarbha (Nam mkha'i snying po) has the perfected ability to purify transgressions.

Akashagarbha is depicted in various poses. He is generally blue in color and clad in azure silk robes. According to one description both his hands are raised at the level of his heart in the gesture of teaching with thumb and index finger touching and the rest of the fingers extended upwards. Between the index finger and thumb of his left hand he holds the stem of a lotus. On the flower, which is level with his left ear, rests a blue sword. He sits cross-legged in the half vajra position with his right foot resting on his left thigh. He is adorned with jewels and looks radiant. He is also depicted riding on a sunbeam with both arms outstretched, palms facing outwards. Behind his right shoulder is the shining orb of the sun.

21. According to Mahayana teaching, no matter how negative an action is, we can cleanse and purify ourselves of it by sincerely applying the four counteractions (*gnyen po stobs bzhi*). These four consist of the power of regret for what we have done (*rnam par sun 'byin pa'i stobs*), the power of the resolve not to repeat that action (*nyes pa las slar ldog pa'i stobs*), the power of the basis (*rten gyi stobs*) and the power of counteractive behavior (*gnyen po kun tu spyod pa'i stobs*). The power of the basis involves taking heartfelt refuge and generating the altruistic intention. It is so called because negative actions are either performed in relation to the Three Jewels—the Buddhas, their teaching and the spiritual community—or in relation to other living beings. We use those towards whom our negative action was directed as a basis for its purification. By taking refuge in the Three Jewels we counteract unwholesome actions performed in relation to them. By arousing the altruistic intention we counteract negative actions performed in relation to other living beings. Anything positive we do with the intention of counter-ing previous negative actions constitutes counteractive behavior.

22. In the fourth chapter of *The Compendium* Shantideva draws on what is said regarding the purification of basic downfalls in the *Akashagarbha Sutra*. He says that those who have created a basic downfall, who fear taking rebirth in one of the bad states and who from the depths of their heart want to see the Bodhisattva

Akashagarbha in order to purify what they have done should act as follows: first they should make three prostrations and call his name. Akashagarbha will then appear to them, taking whatever form accords with their inclination, merit and fortune. The sutra says that he will appear as Brahma, Ishvara, Indra, Sarasvati, as a king, minister, hero, doctor, father, mother, boy or girl or even as a mountain, tree, spring or as the sun or moon.

The basic downfalls created by Bodhisattvas who are still beginners will be purified through this and Akashagarbha will give them both extensive and profound teachings of the Great Vehicle, thereby enabling them to reach the irreversible stages of practice which begin on the path of preparation.

If Akashagarbha does not appear in this way, the Bodhisattva who has committed the transgression should rise in the early hours, well before dawn, face east and, having burnt fragrant incense, should request the son of the gods called First Light as follows: "First Light, First Light, greatly compassionate one, greatly fortunate one, when your radiance falls upon the world, cover me with compassion. Compassionate Akashagarbha, may my words quickly move you to show me in my dreams how to purify my transgressions. And show me how to develop the skillful means and wisdom through which I may attain the exalted paths of the Great Vehicle."

Having made this request, the Bodhisattva should lie down to sleep again and, as light begins to spread over the world, the Bodhisattva Akashagarbha will appear to him or her in dream and will purify the downfall that was created. With consummate expertise Akashagarbha will teach how to develop greater skillful means and wisdom, so that the Bodhisattva who transgressed will develop the meditative stabilizaton of never forgetting the altruistic intention.

23. This always includes taking heartfelt refuge, arousing the altruistic intention, applying the four counteractions and reciting the *Confession Sutra* or performing one of the various purification practices, such as visualization of Vajrasattva and recitation of his hundred-syllable mantra.

24. *Upāyakauśalyasūtra, Thabs la mkhas pa'i mdo*, P927, Vol. 36.

25. Bodhibhadra states that if attachment, anger, pride and so forth are present the faulty action is performed "with disturbing emotions."

Although forgetfulness, laziness and lethargy are classed as secondary disturbing emotions, they are viewed as less grave and for this reason faulty actions accompanied by any of these three are said to have been performed "without disturbing emotions."

Shantarakshita explains that if laziness, which is slothfulness and a lack of interest in the training of Bodhisattvas, is present the faulty action has been performed "with disturbing emotions" but if the transgression occurs out of forgetfulness, it is performed "without disturbing emotions."

Je Tsongkhapa points out that faulty actions performed "with disturbing emotions" are those performed out of greed, lack of contentment, or attachment to reward or respect, when no effort is made to stop these feelings.

26. The words *brtse ba* and *snying brtse* are said to refer to the compassion we feel when we see others suffering, while *snying rje* is said to refer to our feeling of pity when we see someone creating the causes of suffering.

27. This refers to actions that become negative because for certain reasons they have been proscribed (*bcas pa'i kha na ma tho ba*).

28. The four features characterizing the disposition of the exalted (*'phags pa'i rigs bzhi*) are contentment with poor clothing (*chos gos ngan ngon tsam gyis chok shes pa*), contentment with meager alms (*bsod snyoms ngan ngon tsam gyis chok shes pa*), contentment with a poor dwelling (*gnas mal ngan ngon tsam gyis chok shes pa*), and a liking for getting rid of what needs to be discarded and for meditation (*spong ba dang sgom pa la dga' ba*).

29. Actions which are negative not because they have been proscribed but because they are in themselves harmful (*rang bzhin kha na ma tho ba*).

30. The five wrong ways of getting one's livelihood (*log 'tsho lnga*) are: through flattery (*kha gsag*), hinting (*gzhogs slong*), giving something to get something (*rnyed pas rnyed pa 'tshol ba*), for instance by giving something small and hoping to receive something substantial in return, through the use of force (*thob kyis 'jal ba*), and through hypocrisy (*tshul 'chos*).

31. Jetsun Milarepa (Mi la ras pa, Thos pa dga' 1040-1123) is remembered for the many hardships he endured in his devoted efforts to

receive teachings from Marpa (Mar pa lo tsa' ba Chos kyi blo gros, 1012-1097), with whom he stayed for six years and eight months. He is remembered too for his single-mindedness and austere life as a meditator, and for his songs of experience. Of his many disciples the foremost were Rechungpa (Ras chung rDo rje grags, 1083-1161) and Gampopa (sGam po pa, also known as Dvags po lha rje bSod nams rin chen, 1079-1153).

32. Mention of six Buddhas preceding Shakyamuni is found: Vipashyin (rNam gzigs), Shikin (gTsug tor can), Vishvabhu (Thams cad skyob), Krakuchchanda ('Khor ba 'jig), Kanakamuni (gSer thub), and Kashyapa ('Od srung).

33. Good or auspicious signs: *mtshan bzang*.

34. Some versions of the Tibetan text of Chandragomin's *Twenty Verses* read *"byams la lan du phan mi 'dogs,"* which could be taken to mean "not repaying love." However, this is a corruption and the line should read *"byas la lan du phan mi 'dogs."*

35. Many masters of the Kadampa (bKa' gdams pa) tradition were active in Pempo ('Phan po or 'Phan yul), an area to the north of Lhasa, where they established a number of important monasteries.

APPENDIX 1: A TRADITIONAL BIOGRAPHY OF CHANDRAGOMIN

1. This account is drawn from Taranatha's *History of Buddhism in India*, translated by Lama Chimpa and Alaka Chattopadhyaya (Calcutta: K.P. Bagchi & Co., 1970).

2. Nalanda monastic university, in what is now the Indian state of Bihar, was for many centuries the greatest center of secular and Buddhist studies in India. It was founded by King Kumaragupta in the fifth century and was later famed for its outstanding and vast library.

3. Potala hill is said to be where the residence of Avalokiteshvara and Tara is situated on an island in the Indian Ocean. The residence of the Dalai Lamas in Lhasa was named after this. The white Potala palace was constructed between 1645 and 1648. The red Potala palace was begun in 1690 and completed in 1694.

4. The *garuda* (*bya khyung*) is a mythical extremely powerful eagle-like bird, the legendary foe of snakes and nagas.

Source Readings

COMMENTARIES IN TIBETAN THAT SERVED AS A BASIS FOR THIS TEACHING:

sDom pa nyi shu pa'i 'grel ba (*Saṃvaravimśakavṛtti*, P5583, Vol. 114) by Shantarakshita (eighth century)

Byang chub sems dpa'i sdom pa nyi shu pa'i dka' 'grel (*Bodhisattva-saṃvaravimśakapañjikā*, P5584, Vol. 114) by Bodhibhadra (tenth century)

So thar byang sems gsang sngag gsum gyi sdom pa'i bslab bya nor bu'i 'od 'preng, by mTshan zhabs Tshe dbang bsam 'grub (nineteenth century)

Byang chub gzhung lam by Tsong Kha pa, 1357-1419